WAKING DREAMS

Lawrence Sail was born in London and brought up in Exeter. He studied French and German at Oxford University, then taught for some years in Kenya, before returning to teach in the UK. He is now a freelance writer and lives in Exeter.

His retrospective *Waking Dreams: New and Selected Poems* (Bloodaxe Books, 2010) is a Poetry Book Society Special Commendation. It covers work written over four decades, selected from ten collections, from *Opposite Views* (1974) to the *New Poems* (2010) first collected in this book, and draws on four collections previously published by Bloodaxe: *Out of Land: New & Selected Poems* (1992), *Building into Air* (1995), *The World Returning* (2002) and *Eye-Baby* (2006).

His other books include *Cross-currents: essays* (Enitharmon Press, 2005), a memoir of childhood, *Sift* (Impress Books, 2010) and *Songs of the Darkness*, a selection of his Christmas poems with illustrations by his daughter, Erica Sail (Enitharmon Press, 2010). He has edited a number of anthologies, including *The New Exeter Book of Riddles* (1999) and *Light Unlocked: Christmas Card Poems* (2005), both co-edited with Kevin Crossley-Holland for Enitharmon, and *First and Always: Poems for Great Ormond Street Children's Hospital* (Faber & Faber, 1988). He also edited *South-West Review* from 1980 to 1985.

He was chairman of the Arvon Foundation from 1990 to 1994, has directed the Cheltenham Festival of Literature, has been a Whitbread Prize judge, and was the UK jury member for the European Literature Prize (1994-96). In 2004 he received a Cholmondeley Award. He is a Fellow of the Royal Society of Literature.

LAWRENCE SAIL

WAKING DREAMS

NEW & SELECTED POEMS

BLOODAXE BOOKS

Copyright © Lawrence Sail 2010

ISBN: 978 1 85224 883 3

First published 2010 by
Bloodaxe Books Ltd,
Highgreen,
Tarset,
Northumberland NE48 1RP.

www.bloodaxebooks.com
For further information about Bloodaxe titles
please visit our website or write to
the above address for a catalogue.

Supported by
**ARTS COUNCIL
ENGLAND**

Cover design: Neil Astley & Pamela Robertson-Pearce.

Printed in Great Britain by
Bell & Bain Limited, Glasgow, Scotland.

Remembering my parents

Barbara Wright and Hellmut Schmitt

ACKNOWLEDGEMENTS

This book includes poems selected from Lawrence Sail's previous collections: *Opposite Views* (Dent, 1974), *The Drowned River* (Mandeville Press, 1978), *The Kingdom of Atlas* (Secker & Warburg, 1980), *Devotions* (Secker & Warburg, 1987), *Aquamarine* (Gruffyground Press, 1988), *Out of Land: New & Selected Poems* (Bloodaxe Books, 1992), *Building into Air* (Bloodaxe Books, 1995), *The World Returning* (Bloodaxe Books, 2002) and *Eye-Baby* (Bloodaxe Books, 2006).

Acknowledgements are due to the editors of the following publications in which some of the previously uncollected poems first appeared: *English in Education*, *Magma*, *Oxford Magazine*, *Poetry Nation Review*, *Poetry Review*, *The Rialto*, *The Times Literary Supplement* and *The Warwick Review*.

'Edenic' was first published in *A Room to Live in* (Salt Publishing, 2007). 'Portuguese Sonnet' was written to celebrate the opening of a new library in Valença, and included in *Spreading Words* (British Council, 2009). 'Bridget Riley's *Metamorphosis*' was commissioned by the Tate Gallery. 'His Master's Voice' was first published in *Something More than Talk* (Ver Poets, 2006). 'Treading Water' was commissioned by the composer Mark Tanner. 'Overfalls' and 'Undertow' were first published as *Two Sea Poems* by Chestnut Press, 2009. 'A Leaf Falling' was included in a Poems in the Waiting Room pamphlet.

CONTENTS

FROM **OPPOSITE VIEWS**
(1974)

Expatriate Teacher

I bring you the symbols of alien gods
From northern kingdoms weathered by the wind,
Where history lingers, though constantly rewritten
By word and war, by shapely post-war words.

I tell you of illuminated scripts,
The Roman Forum, the statues at Versailles:
Our tendency to build elaborate forms
Beyond our substance, outliving time and pain.

You walk to school barefoot, on stony paths;
By wind-sharp thorn you see the jackal move,
Biding its time. At night the cattle shift
Uneasily beneath the sullen moon.

What use are books and marble, when the senses
Go numb and fail to warn of coming danger?
At home you shed your blazer, casting off
The Latin motto they stitched across your heart.

Death of a Child

It lay beyond the tidy garden ways –
An endless world where wicked berries gleamed
Precisely in the seasonless disorder;
With leaves like flags hoisted to dizzy treetops,
Cables of creeper a foot thick. A place
Where nothing was settled, nothing tamely focused
To prim gravel, a few labelled roses.
He noticed that this area shared with others
The name of 'no', selected by his parents.

The parents, who often later blamed themselves,
Smiled as he tested boundaries through four summers.
The potting shed was good while it lasted, the trees
Easily bore his weight – and when those palled,
It was time to help him make his own small garden:
A replica of father's, ten feet square,
With regular rows and space to walk between.
He liked it when they knelt to dig his garden,
Seeing behind their heads the great space no.

In the fifth year, beneath the splaying orchids,
The opposite view had equal fascination –
Looking back, he could barely define the zone
Of barren ground in which his parents stooped,
Peering, calling, anxious to know where he was.
But he was no, all made of shiny tubers,
With berry eyes and skin smooth as leaves,
Twigs for fingers and a dark mind. In delight
He shouted his name, fled down the unfenced ways.

And when, breathless, he paused, it seemed to him
He stood at his own true threshold – a cool clearing
Of grass and lily flowers, at whose still centre
Bamboo had formed a graceful canopy.
The light still held, he had only to cross.
From the first step forward, he felt the ground give way
In recognition: boldly, with joy, he trod
Into the reed-covered lake. They found him there,
His eyes still bright, staring beyond their world.

The Return

This is the house to which you came back
After your mother died,
These the roseheads pitted with black,
Once her pride.

Here is the door through which you passed
Into the echoing hall
Where gleaming mercury trapped in glass
Predicted rainfall.

Up these stairs which she dusted and swept
Daily, you climbed to bed:
Beside your unwashed pillow, you kept
The book she read.

And this cracked mirror is one in which
Her image beckoned to you
The night they found you drowned in a ditch,
Gazing through.

A Picture by Klee

X-rayed against the double night
Of the cut moon and the dwarf sun,
The wire frames of your skeleton town
Might have been gutted by fire, or nudged
Askew by earthquake.

But over the leaning towers, bright flags
Semaphore their messages
Of occupation, refuse to submit
To natural disaster, or
Random history.

No town was ever so ruined, or sited
So far beyond the reach of weather,
The limits of naming: yet each step taken
Along its deserted streets provokes
Familiar echoes.

For this is the fossil Troy embedded
In all our minds: the child's first sketch
Of heaven, the old man's Holy City,
Clear as glass. The first and last
Possible settlement.

Revival

Nothing escapes me: lying here under the wrappings,
With feet and hands raised to a peak, I share
Each twitch of twilight, can sense the surrounding air
Set gelatine thick with the sweetness of wallflowers, trapping
Drifts of seeds in its finely meshed snare.

Each precious detail homes to my cool tent –
The ringdove gloating in the wood, the tethered rose
Folding itself into sleep; moonlight which glows
Blue in blowball mantles; a dry adjustment
Of wingbones in the snagged and winding hedgerow.

Butterflies wink on my eyelids, wings revive
My sluggish heart. Slowly, whole landscapes infect
Each stretch of tissue. Already I can detect
The lapdog shifting beneath my heels – the live
Tickle of beard across my marble gullet.

FROM **THE DROWNED RIVER**

(1978)

Changing the Clocks

One hour twice yearly is double or quits
for Doctor Faustus: on the stroke of two
the old régime is toppled in
a bloodless coup.

Prim hands reach up, correcting clock-hands,
and here it comes or goes, the hour
in which the darkest seeds of dreaming
might fully flower.

All sixty minutes stuffed with wishes!
The eleventh hour is tenth or twelfth,
Cinders walks home, or the prince advances
with lustful stealth.

And twice a year we draw back curtains
on light and darkness re-arranged,
see birds above old towers migrating
and time unchanged.

Old Man Exploring

There is no threshold:
the front swings open
entire, revealing
the model of a mind
unhinged to cross-section
at one blow of the knife.

Here in remembrance
no candles are lit:
though the unstarred stems
stand ready, each petite
compartment is its own
dream of dead reckoning.

21

Nowhere a footfall
or echo, only
immaculate dust
settled on Lilliput,
on its inch-long tables,
its chairs half an inch high.

Somewhere in these cells
lies the point at which
a sense of pattern
overcame the senses:
a room where I may find
sunlight, or rats feasting.

On Porlock Beach

Do it once more. Lob the stone
you have just chosen – a layered chip
of Siena cathedral, green and whitish,
pummelled by pressures greater than Gothic –
and see it slither, mix to the mile-long
shelf of the foreshore.

Gone for ever – and no other stone
its exact equal. For sense you scan
the broader background, the curve of cliffs,
sea setting; eager to interpret
the laws of rhythm somewhere short
of never-never.

You harangue your heart, but cannot quench
a drowning desire to sense the single
in calm collectives; to let the beach
be each budding stone landing and lodging –
as judgements, whole with luck, but at least
tested by their parts.

In the Trout Hatchery

1

Superfluous now the upstream gravel
of redds cut clean, the drift of milt:
this river has no story, travels
a table's length, mouths into buckets
and spills away. Sky is a tilt
of dark and starless wood.
Conceived to order, these need no luck.

They harbour their plans. Beneath the skin,
black pips for eyes: each berry stores
enough to last two months of waiting.
As soft as ticks, pre-human, apart,
they glow with knowledge, calmly adoring
the quiet circles of time.
In time, they panic the human heart.

2

Black inches spate
beneath the wheel
which regulates
the fall of feed –
a printer's tray
of twitching marks
bumping and turning
through light and dark,
gold-eyed greed.

You gladly shift
your gaze to where
a few fish drift
calmly – one yaws
in rings, its spine
a rigid bend;
eyeless, another
comes to an end
blindly in jaws.

Between two fears
your mind demands
a choice: but here
in one long line
the equal water
shines and shines.

Trees Uprooted

All their slow experience
one well-aimed gust has skittled down:
suddenly they are back among
dwarf torments, the crawling pressures
they emigrated from.

Falling, still their wrenched roots
closed fists on earth's bright underside,
levering lids of chalk and peat
head-high: in the death-bed hollows
the alien sunlight seethes.

Spring arrives with mad trophies
to wreathe the headstones: bluebells shoot
sideways from six feet up, new fern
spills down into air. Wild flowers
are drowned in falling sap.

Nothing, then, in the gone wind's shaft,
but rounds of chalk propped up on poles
crumbling in summer rain and heat:
moons mouthing through swathes of shadow
the lasting O of echo.

FROM **THE KINGDOM OF ATLAS**
(1980)

Alphabet Soup

The sunken letters keep their options,
scarcely evolved in a soapy broth
where the last word on any subject
melts to an anagram of moonshine,
literal truth.

No given usage quite wears them out:
consumed, they might be the sacrament
of pride swallowed – or, stirred, resettle
oh in omens, telling the future
in new last words.

Innocent as messengers they stand
by, are only bearers of the word –
already looking elsewhere, as we
try to break the rosy seals, to get
at real meaning.

Children in Snow

White fritterings,
the hedges pasted high
with glue: and the land drifting
up to a darkness which flares
like blue gas at the rim.

Our children step
easily into it:
too small for comparisons
they ride absolutes simply,
printing with their red boots.

In the distance
we see them jerk and slip,
fooled by the least tip of slope:

delighted dwarves, they welcome
each new loss of balance.

Beaded curtains
fall between them and us.
They will come back, we are sure.
If we shout, then they will come,
red-cheeked and with bright eyes.

They cross borders
without even knowing:
one day, will be beyond
recall, all trace of them thawed
into valleys, green hills.

Post-Operative

Not a cut but a wound
the doctors always called it –
as if wanting to say
that no unkindness was meant,
but also that, besides bleeding,
it would cause hurt too.

Not a cut but a wound –
so that, three years after,
when at night our son sings
bravely to himself for hours,
his mother still sighs and says,
'He is afraid. He remembers.'

And when, rubbing him dry,
I brush the ridge of scar,
I wince and search his eyes
for evidence not of a cut
but a wound that will not heal.
'Shall I sing to you?' I ask.

Swimmer Returning

Ahead of me the waves went in
repeating lunar influence
steadily on the beach where stones
clustered like boxed eggs.
Lapped in the wide grooves of the sea
I was all passive, worked upon –
prickled by sunlight, my lips washed
by a dribble of salt, fingers
rubbed loose, wrinkled by water.

Miles of coastline rode at my eyes:
towns with their model frontages
remaindered under hills, high fields
drifting to the edge
of land as simply sliced away
as a piece of cake. And above,
great bluffs of cloud, unmoving floss,
signalled that nothing here could be
the least problematical.

Then, arrival at the shallows
where to swim becomes a pretence:
reluctantly I evolved through
ninety degrees, stood
in abrasive air. I recall
being startled by my own height,
as I shook the sea from my feet
and limped up the sharp slope, each step
now loaded with gravity.

At night I lie flat on my back,
hoisted to high exile above
the city's unending systems.
Half a mile away
the river smacks its concrete lips,
and I dream of the view waiting
at its last turn: the simple sea
waxed by moonlight, the dark dot
of a head bobbed on the waves.

Old Woman at Threshold

On one hand the hall
where everything is arranged –
a feather of a plant leaning
from a turban of polished brass,
my favourite white gloves ready
as always on the small table
and, by the handrail greased with light,
stairs mounting to darkness.

On the other hand
young grass in its hoop of iron
thriving, buds once more triumphant,
the sundial twisting shadows
round its pointed finger: and then
the privet wall with the square gap
where traffic blurs by, and walkers
always stay in profile.

And I stand between,
balancing on this shrinking ledge,
mad châtelaine of the threshold,
with hair wired tight all round the brain
in which I hear the rising scream
no agency of care or love
can monitor, as the dead weight
of two lost worlds moves in.

Time Machines

1

In shady transepts
the hustle of cogs
meshes exactly,
their battled teeth
strong enough
to crush bone
where gaps meet.

Time pinked out
in a dry two-step
bites on air,
each turn of a tick
nibbling the old
canonical hours
to fractions of fear.

2

Eternity teeming
in a figure of eight
collapses into
its own reflection –
a growing pyramid
of uncountable grains
whose sly fall
stifles the ground.

Without a sound
it climbs glass walls
to silt the brain
and boil eggs solid –
a soft infection
filtering through
lives which too late
I remember dreaming.

3

Beneath events, each thousand years
distils to an inch of closing jaws.
In the deep cave, our hearts bursting
with pain or love could hardly fill
one drop
falling to darkness.

But here is time as the heart loves it:
a conjuror's trick, the empty half
of the spangled box where history lay
to be cut in two. From that hollow cave
whole lifetimes
rise to sunlight.

Shakespearian Seascape

Out of the timeless ocean,
that other, uncrammed O,
you conjure your characters –
their bones made of coral,
with eyes which once were pearls.
Passengers on a ship
manned by jokers, they feel
the first gulp of breath,
their hearts beginning to quicken.

A hand smoothes the chart:
your impresario's finger
points to the scarlet Gulf Stream,
then, farther south, picks out
the hulls of a fleet near Cyprus –
and there, another, reforming
offshore from Actium.
Elsewhere a single boat
limps through a freak storm.

A long, long voyage
and at the end no place
except one island, sufficient
to allow a last enactment
of what the truth demands.
Here, within earshot
of the waves, nothing can heal
but magic and terra firma,
Gonzalo's sense of the real.

Moonstruck in your wake,
we wonder at such words
breaking the darkness – endless
pirated editions
of possible lives made fact.
Evolving through rich tropics
from the sea-bed's shifting ground,
we share that hope of land,
of only seeming to drown.

The Kingdom of Atlas

1

Along the flickering wake
of sunset, the waves glitter
as wickedly tempered as
those cusps of glass which protrude
from the long jaws of my walls.

For this is my rounded realm,
the lethal half-life of fear
enclosed in ring after ring –
the sea hemming the island,
the island warded with walls,
walls which go round the orchards,
orchards which keep the apples,
apples whose cores hold the seeds
of fear, its lethal half-life
enclosed in ring after ring.

The time will come when my words
are all drowned in one echo,
echo which never, never
stops, however quietly,
repeating *the time will come*.

2

My herds wander on the hills,
my flocks drink from wide water,
the obedient serpent
hugs the tree, and my children
flourish, their skin soft as milk.

Surely the gods will honour
the maintenance of beauty,
the work of custodians?
I clear the highest gutters
blocked up by the spiteful birds,
I smoke out the deepest mole
at the first lift of the ground.

I am alert to the least
danger, and I know just how
laburnum tempts the children.

But the gods also excel
in irony, who made me
lord of earth's furthermost shores:
possessed, I watch the needy
steal up to my minded doors.

3

The world's weight rests on my stem –
lying snug between the skull
and its axis, I support
every shade of opinion,
each gesture of agreement.

I am the fixed point from which
all mapping begins, from where
the lie of the land reveals
its daily experience,
the true value of naming,
the consolations of truth.
Knowing my legend by heart
you will not mistake your path
and may even find in time
the way to welcome strangers.

For this too is my kingdom,
where music may bring down walls
and blossom break from waste ground:
where even now the echo
in your head is a brand-new sound.

Hammock Journeys

Inbending,
a hoisted foetus,
you entertain
all possible worlds
except the possible
call from the house;
preferring time,
like disbelief, suspended.

Humming,
you swing, a trophy
bagged and slung
between dark trees
which shoulder you home
through elephant grass;
the English summer
throbs to exotic drums.

Making
great lolling leeway,
your rope canoe
leaks yellow diamonds,
the parasol paddle
trails astern;
sinking, you glimpse
weed on a high blue lake.

Dozing
is vague awareness
of hands being folded,
of the narrow pillow
propping the head,
of coins of light
heavy on eyes;
earth, rich earth is close.

The Meat Commission, Kenya

Beached upcountry
it rides the hills,
all cabins lit,
a frantic steamer
waving the flag
of its fine name.

Daily the cattle
replenish the ark,
nodding to their death
in a shroud of dust,
fruit of the plain's
long seasons.

And daily the knife
divides and discards:
horn and hoof
rattle down chutes,
tinned flesh
glints in the railyards.

In how many places
with fine names
have sleeves been rolled
above blood level,
even in the name
of our salvation?

Night and day
the maribous wait
and, trembling, adore
the curdled air.
Their endless appetites
burden the trees.

The Drinking Songs of Attila

1

What makes a city?
The stink of defeated nomads.
What makes a borough?
Saddles cracked with age.
What makes a township?
Women's voices blockading
thresholds with their patient rage.

What makes a suburb?
Tents frozen into gables.
What makes a ghetto?
Power in the wrong hands.
What makes a village?
Brittle ploughshares, dividing
acres of divided land.

What makes for freedom?
Ah, the answer to that,
my feckless burghers,
is hidden somewhere between
my hollow cheek
and your rictus grins.

2

I give you deserted garage forecourts
and the endless grammar of grey crescents.
I give you double glazing, and miles
of regular religious hedges.
I give you the last recorded minutes
of the last committee to be impaled
on points of order with a cutting edge:
drink with me to their open options!

Think of the mannered groves of learning
stiff with gas, the faculties
besieged by panic. Think of the children
penning their sour memoirs in words
they scribble on graveyard walls. Think

of the Legion of the Lark, on the east border,
unpaid for months, still oiling their swords:
drink with me to their open options!

3

I drink to the homage of Hollywood,
to fables bright as a Chinese parrot –
Attila the baddie, Attila the good –
to the propaganda of brazen trumpets
calling the armies once again
to conflicts easily understood –
Attila the monk plays Attila the hood.

Gentlemen, is it too late
to remember those who survived?
Is it not thanks to me
that Venice came to rise
on the shores of a tame sea?
My scarlet music was wiser
than any guarded gate.

4

Remember also the Danube as it was
on the day of my wedding and of my death –
cusps of brightness riding the flow,
the mist drifting like a slow breath...
Bullshit! I've often turned my back
on more exquisite gloom than that.
I give you instead the god I made
in your own image: the settling dregs
of all my golden hero's dreams.

The Auction Rooms

Daily, in the undertaker's clearing-house,
money is nodded away in vague exchange
for sleepwalkers' bargains, the crazy household
of job lots quite impervious to fashion.
Here in the last redoubt of manufacture
outrageous curiosity can redeem
anything wheeled out of a burning city
or lacking appeal to cool inheritors.

In time, almost everything goes: but never
bedlinen. Never that – a single night's use
seems infection enough. Month on month it grows,
a hill rusted with iron-mould, a pale taboo
whose stiff slopes of Turin microfilm enfold
the privately printed history of death.

The Keyboard in C Major

No reaching forward,
no reaching up:
all that you offer
is the music which Faust
laughed at in the womb,
the toothsome sweetness
of the prodigal's return
caving into
a succession of days,
his coming of age.

Your Italian gifts
are all-white serenities
no one could bear
but for the shadows
which swell about you:

and those who love you
are those who still hope
for tumultuous dreams
of apotheosis
or shrieking damnation.

Poem for a Cinema Organist

Fifteen years ago you sank
in glorious bars of purple light,
your silver hair
a landmark where
an era disappeared from sight.

Now, as unpredictably,
you surface here, inside a school,
to intercede
in sloppy tweeds
for all things bright and beautiful.

Metronomic fingers wag
around the old harmonium –
when pleasure's gone
God's antiphon
is what the prodigal becomes.

God be praised, at your first touch
usherettes tap-dance down the aisles,
improving quatrains
melt to profane
Savoy arpeggios, wicked style.

Sparkling syncopations guard
the faith you've kept while growing older –
while angels hum
the rainbow comes
to curve its colours at your shoulder.

At Rye

(for Patric Dickinson)

The facts are brilliantly alleged –
famous residents, antique streets,
the glaze of earthenware – and all
infer the statute hoisted above
the church: *for our time is a very shadow*
that passeth away. Flanking the text,
the quarterboys smirk in their gilt fat.

And two miles south, a plausible sea
unwinds as it should onto a beach
of shells milled to shards of bone.
Where neaps and springs quarter the days,
shifting their mane of sticky kelp
across the shore, who could contest
the evidence of time passing?

Appearances smooth as an alibi –
But here at the town's brink, the cliff
insists on posing for the perfect cadence
only water could hope to complete.
Within its shadow, houses and meadows
laid in the wake of the absent sea
are inadmissible, pure illusion.

Into that zone no facts can cover,
real as the oldest hopes of love
or the sag left in my father's chair,
the ocean floods back, beating like blood,
proof against time. At night I feel it
lapping at my mind, where the quiet triumphs
of the dead are borne in on a rising tide.

The Age of Reason

At the twelfth hour
when two was two
and all alone
and lightning had struck
the struck tree,

when by some seventh sense
a magnificent cat
was stretching at the door
of its tenth life
in five-leafed clover,

then, as the wedding guests
were presenting their knives,
some fool remembered
the date – Saturday
the unlucky fourteenth.

Eating Maize

From the very first it has been
a history of destructions:
the long leaves wincing,
silky tassels torn away
from buttery knuckles clenched
as tightly as a grenade.

Year after year I suck
the sweet and yellowed bone
of rich summer, teeth
burrowing inwards until
the racks are hollow, and I hold
nothing but tough litter.

Then I dream how with one
long and careful cut
I might find, inside the core,
a whole hillside crackling
with head-high plantations,
acres of solid fruit.

Supreme illusionist,
I can recreate hope
endlessly, like a set
of gleaming Russian dolls
by Caesarian section
out of a single season.

Yet from the first it was
a history of destructions:
in winter I see myself
as an old but never replete
cannibal, eating my heart out
with a terrible hunger for innocence.

South Yorkshire

Transactions seethe from cooling-towers
deep in submissive meadows wormed
with stopcocks, fine filters, bolted pipes.
Fat reservoirs of old habits,
like dazed relics the cattle confront
light retreating to a raw line
along canals. On every side
strictest codes enjoin the landscape.

To each village its gothic dogma,
the low skyline buttressed at pits
with black lattices, wheels which decline
day and night in a flick of spokes.
To each mine its ragged pentecost
of flame held high into the wind,
proclaiming from lips greasy with soot
that work is love, a sacred cow.

But canny, orthodox old women
keep to their cramped parlours, obsessed
with cleanliness, and not forgetting
their younger selves already bent
double all the day long, collecting
tatties to earn a beggar's wage:
still they wonder at the pure paleness
of those nuggets prised from dark soil.

They take for emblem the turned thumbful
of white oilpaint gleaming above
the power-plant stack: that, at their death,
they too may rise, a clean harvest
hatched from the diocese of dust –
in dreams, seeing how their clear blood
might blossom from broken pipes to bless
the fields, revoke all heresies.

Shells

Along the banded beach
lie tellins, bright crash-landed butterflies,
with shells of mussels, blue and glossy almonds,
and scallops, fossil fans laid out to dry.
Shells, like words, are what you make of them –
pilgrims' badges, money, pubic shields,
Aztec tribute, scoops for holding oil,
pastry moulds or gems.

To match the shining fragments
or find the metaphor of a different use
appears retrieval of a kind, but brings
no sense of shape: the bits remain diffuse
as waves are in the sparkling air of distance.
Beneath the minded phrases, what remains
is half a story, lifeless beauty shrugged
off by tides, a clearance.

Imagination learns
to work at absences, to re-invent
the valves of stranded swimmers, burrowers, borers,
their slimy hearts, their palps and ligaments –
and only then may hope to see, salt-fresh,
the ocean purling tamely at her heels,
Aphrodite as she is, a resurrection
not of words but flesh.

FROM **DEVOTIONS**
(1987)

Snooker Players

They whistle the fine smoke
Of blue dust from the cue,
Suave as gunslingers, never
Twitching one muscle too few.
At ease, holstering their thumbs
In trimmest waistcoats, they await
Their opponent's slip, the easiest
Of shots miscalculated.
Their sleek heads shine, spangled
With the sure knowledge of every angle.

Once at the table, they bend
In level reverence to squint
At globe after globe, each
With its window of light glinting
On cushioned greener than green,
The rounded image of reason.
One click and cosmology thrives,
All colours know their seasons
And tenderly God in white gloves
Retrieves each fallen planet with love.

Watching them, who could believe
In the world's lack of balance?
Tucked in this pocket of light
Everything seems to make sense –
Where grace is an endless break
And justice, skill repaid,
And all eclipses are merely
A heavenly snooker displayed.
Yet all around, in the framing
Darkness, doubt dogs the game.

Allotments

(for Charles Causley)

Since time continues to demand its bleak honours,
let them be awarded here, where thrift cuts wastage
to a minimum – old elixirs corked with rag
in sheds as close and devotional as chantries –
where each new year the gaudy seed-packets signal
the resurrection of hope, and by grass duckboards
the twine unwinds to love in its fruiting season.

The allotments have become their own aerial view –
the land as it appears in the gunner's reticle,
squared into simple plots, as a god might see it,
familiar yet strange, the workings of creatures
who seem to believe, but almost as a hobby:
and always the same workings, set at the edges
of every railway journey and of dark canals.

Even the ornaments recur – the upturned bowls
riddled with couch-grass, or the bicycles leaning
at a post, or the smoke rising in unison
from autumn fires, or the clack of spades resounding,
or the soft shifting of sieves. Here time will run out
endlessly, but can never defeat the tenants
of the last real estate of common prayer.

At Possenhofen

(for John Mole)

The meadow in its mildness stretches on
And on beside the waters of the lake
Whose shallows, cloudy as kaolin, support
Boat after boat saluting to the breeze.

Games are played, bright frisbees slice the air,
Children run about, fall and get up again.
Blue smoke drifts by from meat being burnt.
People are idly kissing and talking and jigging
Up and down by rubber dugouts, blowing
With their feet; or lying pegged out on little jetties
Which sacrifice them to the fiery summer sun.
Many also are swimming, close to some swans.

They have discovered an African freedom from scale,
Each has escaped to become a function of all –
All the brown bodies, the simple vanities
Of dark brown breasts and the swanky male bulge,
Or the strip of bikini swooping down between legs
To grip the minimal groin and shout, like that one
There, in fluorescent green, 'Look at my tan!' –
A whole species on holiday from hermeneutics.

As if history had no value but accretion,
Were really just a mad king or two building castles
In Spain or Bavaria, then quietly drowning,
Each in his own dark lake. But every garden
Of earthly delights will conjure the triumph of death:
Beyond the wood, the railway runs straight past
Brueghel's Spanish soldiery to soul's north,
That other nakedness, those other fires.

In today's breeze, boat after boat nods:
Beside the lake the meadow stretches on
South of Dachau. Here nobody sees more
Than what they see. No one mentions God.

Reichert's Leap

(In December 1911, Walter Reichert, a self-employed
tailor, attempted to fly from the Eiffel Tower)

Each hopeless stitch homemade – the futile skin
Out of which he would jump. It's too late now,
Even if he wanted, as surely he must be wanting,
To climb down. He crouches on the cold brow
Of madness, on the parapet's fine brink,
His breath smearing the air, an unused silence
Which might have been saving speech. *Here, what do you think?*
I didn't mean it. Of course. It makes no sense.
Or simply, *We'll have a drink and then I'll go*
To embrace my poor wife and children. Later, we'll chat.
Too late. They say the journalists wouldn't throw
Their story out of the window, and that was that.
He shifts like a bird – ridiculous, he fears.
Go on, you're chicken. He cannot, will not stay
For this. A puff of looping breath. The sheer
Drop. The stupid tower begins to sway
In his mind only. A final shuffle and
A plop as into water. The deficient air
Fails to support him. A black duster lands,
Bundles into the ground. A brief affair.
Men in caps. Fuss. A canvas shroud.
A way elbowed through the encroaching crowd.

Which of us, from our tower, would not recall
This brute parabola of pride and fall? –
Late Romantics, fledgling birdmen all.

Boatman Shot

Reading it in the paper, it seemed quite simple –
The Times correspondent, coming to a lake
In northern El Salvador, had wanted to cross
With five other newsmen, in order to discover
Whether the army, American-trained, had killed
Some peasants in land the guerrillas controlled. Old story.

San Nicolás, the hamlet in the story,
Was just that, its people plain and simple –
As was the evidence that the army had killed
Possibly more than a hundred. Back on the lake
The boat sank, leaving the travellers to discover
Their own way home, with a day's jungle to cross.

Back in San Salvador, in the shadow of the cross,
The boatman tasted whisky, went the story,
For the first time ever, and was happy to discover
What kept the newsmen going. He found it simple –
Just as it had been to ferry them over the lake
And find the villagers whom the soldiers had killed.

Two days after, the National Guard, who killed
For a living, came and took the boatman to cross-
Examine him about the foreigners at the lake
And about his part in a bad news story
Implying abuse of human rights. It was simple –
The truth, they said, was all they wanted to discover.

Finally they released him, unable to discover
The truth of what had happened, or who had killed
The villagers. The boatman, back in his simple
House, began to realise that to cross
From one shore to another was a story
Which had its hidden depths, just like the lake.

Too late he glimpsed the figures rising from the lake,
Some dressed like soldiers, in green. They did not discover
Anything worth listening to in his story.
They took the boatman out of his house and killed
Him then and there. His widow bears the cross
Of seven children. The future looks very simple.

Suchitlan was the lake, Alas the boatman killed.
This poem is his, who discovered and ferried across
The necessary truth, keeping the story simple.

African Moments

1

What the sun most brightly shines on
is not the Presidential Suite
not the Hotel Continental
not the cinema's cool plush depths
not the taxidermist's trophies
not the straw of packing-cases
not the traffic lights and meters
not the haze of the loud bazaar
but the puddle bright as tin
beneath the slum's one public tap
from which water slowly dripping
discharges all the wanton seeds
of hope which ride inside the belly
of every Trojan horse of a city.

2

Our host, apologetic, indicates
wood and canvas buckled on the verandah,
a torn rainbow of colours, with stiff limbs
wrecked at all angles – and, tight-lipped, explains,
'Damned hyenas, at the deck-chairs again.'

Later, when the boy has cleared and gone,
he sighs a little, adding that he thinks
all history is really very simple.
Enter the tyrants, shouldering deck-chairs:
the people howl with laughter in their lairs.

Runners, Fading

(for Matthew)

How long ago was it
when they broke from the line
at crazy speed, urged on
by the fear of not fitting
that first hedge-gap?

Before the race, waiting,
they had looked pitiful,
much too clumsy, their legs
too gawky, the black numbers
pinned on askew.

Standing, sucking their breath
and ignoring ahead,
they let their feet stutter
on wet grass. One or two tried
to tell a joke.

Then they were off, upping
and downing and jostling,
slowly spreading, starting
to move less up and down, more
smoothly along.

They have gone now, fading
into distance like a
new dimension, beyond
recognition: and we wait
as if for forgiveness.

Slumped, an obvious parent,
inside the steamed-up car,
I long to hear the plimp
of feet on tarmac: to see
you, returning.

Dreaming of My Father

Up and up together we went
Through the rich, narrow garden,
Me and my father. A steep ascent
And the stairs of grass were hard,
Filled in. He was leaving at last.
Ja, ja, die Treppe, he murmured,
Smiling, recalling the interred
Treads of the hollow past.

As we climbed, he began to reveal
The names of flowers: once he paused
To admire the progress of seeds sealed
In candy-stripe drinking-straws.
Twice, softly, he spoke my name –
But each time he did so, I heard
The voice of my stepmother – an absurd
Acoustic trick, I thought, or a game.

I looked at him, then realised:
This time *he* had lived longer.
Although he looked very tired, his eyes
Were just as blue as when, much younger,
He had ridden a donkey right through Crete,
His jacket loose about his shoulders,
Self-consciously handsome, and so bold
He had looked almost immune to defeat.

And now, gently, he was reciting
The names of all the plants that stood
In a warm hutch, the last on the right,
On a long shelf of wood.
They grew on dolls'-house teapots
Whose lids were turned upside-down –
And every single one
Was a kind of forget-me-not.

An Incident in Kent

(for Elinor Moore)

My daughter, at six, almost drowned
At a swimming pool in Kent, at a school.
It was nobody's fault – she had been in already,
Had dressed and returned and was bending down
To splash a friend who was still in the pool
When suddenly in she went, head

Over heels. As quickly the friend dived
To get her. That was all. Soon after,
She learned to swim. For her, what stays
Vivid is not the shock of revival
But two boys and their unkind laughter
At seeing her baptised, buried and raised.

For me, what stays is what she said
At the time, hardly retrieved, gasping:
I knew I was safe because I could see
The water there above my head.
Words that might have been her last
Or locked in her throat for eternity –

And I think of Hugo at Soubise, sitting down
In a café with his mistress, ordering beer
And opening a paper without any foreboding
To read of his daughter's death by drowning –
His face and his hair were wet with tears.
His poor hand was pressed to his heart as though...

The rest of the story could hardly mean
More than post-mortem – the early mist,
The lightness of the dinghy, which made them ship
Two stones as ballast: Léopoldine
Changing her mind, unable to resist
Her husband's smile or the thought of the trip.

At Caudebec, yet more stones
To reassure cautious Maître Bazire,
The lawyer. Then, after a lull,
A sudden gust. All the weight thrown
To one side. Capsize. No help near.
Didine clinging for a time to the hull...

The mother sat, fingering strands
Of the drowned girl's hair, hour after hour.
She kept her red-checked dress to dote on,
Folded in a bag. With trembling hand,
I loved that poor child beyond my power
To express in words, the poet wrote.

What else could he write, but that the grass
Must grow, and children die – what do,
But volley the blanks of guilt and grief
At a God who had fallen to black farce?
What words, what art could see him through
To any believable kind of belief?

He could not help himself: each year
He wrote a poem for the rose-planted grave,
Phrase after phrase still keenly edged –
Till somehow he re-invented the world
Of love, by imagining being there: saved
By seeing the water above his head.

Fable

He found a stone shaped like a heart
On a rattling beach, in the last spring
His parents shared. It needed no art,
Felt heavy, had good colouring,
Would pass for real, or once real, rather.
Smiling, he gave it to his father.

That summer she found a stone like a hand
In a stream, and on it painted a sleeve,
Black buttons, a white cuff and
One accusing finger leaving
No room for doubt, or little, rather.
She thought it would amuse her father.

Their father built a house of stones
Which, polished and angled, could skim the light
In rooms where now he lived alone.
Perhaps the children thought to write,
Perhaps he, with his hand on his heart,
Would swear he could feel the haemhorrhage starting.

Hallowe'en Lantern

In the darkness, a face, skull-nosed,
Saw-toothed, slit-eyed – each year
A child's wild one-man show
Of root savagery would glow
At the window, in a rough blur.

Its soft brain, very neatly
Gouged, spooned clean away,
Had left its crass top completely
Ill-fitting, a soup-pot where sweetly
The smell of burning stayed.

Crackling waxily, profane,
Neckless, a drunken dome,
It stood between curtain and pane
Facing the frost or the dark rain
Through which I shivered home.

My mind's a blank. What went on
Behind that grin, in those banging
Rooms which belong to no one?
My children will go, my wife has gone –
In the darkness I see a face, hanging.

Rocamadour

What light concealed, the darkness brings to light:
Seventy times seven, the human urges
Ranked in melting turrets, the wavering verges
Stacked in hope against the soul's dark night.

A fakir's bed of nails, on which to lay
An antidote to fear or to regret:
I wish, I wish – each tallow pronoun sweats
Its limited plea into the iron tray.

Across the walls, the proof in solid stone,
A gallery of favours, faith rewarded:
Row after row of triumph, thanks recorded
To the Black Virgin, who sits upon her throne

With Jesus perched on the edge of her left knee.
Angular, rigid, candle-flames catching the lights
In her crown – her eyes turned inward, blank as night,
Demanding everything, blind with certainty.

I lit a candle, too, and followed you out,
Hoping you had not seen. *Oh please, oh please* –
Clean as the mouth of a tunnel, that doorway cleaving
The darkness of faith and the pale day of doubt.

English Versions

This is the English year's translation of sorrow –
A failed late May, in which tense families walk
Through dripping avenues of rhododendrons
Where rain has washed the flowers to mortal paleness.
Hearts ache by the dark, peaty lake, its surface
More wrinkled than a prune.

No horizon looks through into tomorrow,
but somewhere a smooth political voice keeps talking –
'Spend! Spend! Spend!' It bleakly booms, intent on
Drowning despair. In a flapping marquee, for sale,
Dogged home produce, damp books. A draw takes place
For remaindered June.

And here is the English calendar's rendering of bliss –
The uncut grass of wildly catholic meadows
Stained blue and red, beneath the massy heights
Of candled chestnuts: a sweetness of May air
That only lovers could hope to multiply
In naked heat.

Nothing conceivably could be added to this:
Faith is a static heat-haze, neither to nor fro,
Simple as the switchback lanes hemmed in so lightly
By cloudy drifts of cow-parsley. Overhead, somewhere,
June begins in a far calm lake of sky
Where sun and moon meet.

Boxers

Between these twanging staves
Is only the bell's one-two –
Clock, Farewell or Surprise,
The crowd's cheers or boos.

Above the glossy shorts
They've only the silk of sweat
And the blank grin that tries
To camouflage pain and regret.

They must keep dancing, keep
Those kidneys, cherry-red,
On the attack, or begging
Close into the head.

They must keep dancing, must
Avoid those double figures –
But such directness, in time,
Will take its toll of vigour:

Like passionate lovers they
Will tangle in the end,
And gently be eased apart
By their natty mutual friend.

Yet they allow those men
In the corners to give them stick
Till they wince, to sponge them, send them
Back to face the music.

Long before it's over
They want an end to harm,
To fall, *ponderoso*,
Into each other's arms.

But blood is blood and, besides,
They can hear through the smoky din
That voice which is always waiting
On the far side of any win:

You're only just as good, son,
As you are in your next bout –
Darkness and common time,
And the bell ringing down and out.

Two Figures

Dart is deaf and digs the garden strip:
He wears blue trousers with a slick city stripe.
With them manacled to his legs he reaches the house
On a clicking bicycle heavy as any horse.
He wields the pump as if he wants to knock
The stuffing out of you. He also may take knick-knacks
That take his eye. Sometimes he asks to be fired.
Once he hurled a brick at our hired black Ford.
He talks to himself and seems to be quite at home.
His wife, seen once, is somehow part of him –
In curlers, with funny eyes and very short,
And a floral apron over a man's shirt.

And Membury the dwarf who lives just short
Of the thundering trains which every so often shoot
Smoke from the cutting up in a ragged fan –
Membury yellow as the *Beano* and *Radio Fun*
In his front window, who really wears gaiters and hoards
All his money in a large tin box which he hides.
His darkened parlour smells equally of cats,
Newsprint and pee. Not even *Comic Cuts*
Has anyone to beat him. His piping voice,
Absurdly shrill, seems caught in some mad vice:
He tries and tries to clear his little throat,
Nervous as a lizard, as if afraid of threats.

Both long dead – but here they come, unhurried,
The dark grotesques of vivid childhood fears,
Spotless in detail, arcing over the years,
Harbingers of all not dead, just buried.

Nude Coming Downstairs

(after Duchamp)

I am not this one or that one,
Here or now, then or when –
I am a multiple negative,
Never cancelling myself,
Not going upstairs.

I am not anything as simple
As the central figure: I've tried.
Even my sex is unclear,
I am so clad in movement,
So decently blurred.

For all I know, we might have
Stepped clean off the roundabout
Somewhere between maybe
And has-been, but forgetting nothing,
Expecting everything still.

One of us has to decide
What to do when we reach
The hall: how best to greet
Anyone who might be waiting
With flowers for me, for me.

The Lady Chapel, Long Melford

Uncarved by age
the white stones
bandage my eyes
soft as milk
the walls make
to lap at my soul

Behind me death
is a simple door
of grey wood
the worms have made
light as a comb
of drifting sponge

Nothing here
could be learned or looted
it is only something
fallen into
from long acceptance
accrued joy

Cool as in a dairy
the air hoards
unskimmed light
without fuss
all the books
have been put aside

The clock keeps nothing
but nursery time
each hour
one level chime
taps on the shoulder
and soon is gone

And from the numbers
set in the wall
the ghosts of children
multiply
their singing way
to white infinity

The white stones
bandage my eyes
soft as milk
the walls make
to lap at my soul
with mother-love

Apologia

Such riddling quiddities, such suppositions!
Men say that Christ at least was in the world,
Even if not of it; while we have turned
Our backs, in order to practise our devotions –
A narrow virtue barely squeezed between
Addiction and indulgence. Do they think
I twitch blindly through from matins and lauds
To compline and the silence? I know as well
As any man which army's where, or how
To bind a beggar's sores, or what is meant
By swelling in the groin, or gobs of blood.

Lately I did the Psalms – and still like best
The first – the blessing in *Beatus* given
In stem and branch, a pair of crouching lions,
Birds and a cat's mask, the whole most richly done
With vine and oak leaves, brightened with acanthus.
Now, it's the Gospels: on a ground of green,
Light blue and lavender, the drops of gold
Lifted with care across the smooth, ruled vellum.
L for Matthew, already done, then I
For Mark, Q for Luke, then I again
For John – red ivy, with columbine, I think...

I do not pretend, as the truly ruthless do,
That any pain can be contracted to fit
The fluency of words or shining paint –
Or that the world's my cloister. All my art,
Beneath rich foliage, curling metaphor,
Commutes between God's world and the Trappist heart.
Yet what is learned in silence needs its say –
Next year, if I am spared, I hope to start
On a new challenge, my first Book of Hours.
I shall include St Martin and the Beggar,
And the Virgin helping St Thomas to mend his shirt.

The Escaped Names

He who strives for the escaped names brings to consciousness others
JUNG

Under the cover of light, the words we choose,
The others have long since gone: and of those that remain,
Which can tell us now their original meanings?
Each venture, it seems, is an old beginning
With equipment so shot and gone that no one would think
Of staging a raid. Or, in another translation,
Lovely enchanting language, sugar-cane,
Honey of roses, whither wilt thou fly?

No end, of course, to our vocabularies,
Evasion after evasion – but who will compile
A dictionary beyond the reach of random,
The impossible esperanto which no one speaks
But all believe in? If we were fluent in that,
Surely those ancestral words would still be waiting
In the echoing belly of the horse, in the old city,
Where now there is only moonlight and scattered stone.

Meanwhile, since there must by definition
Be always at least two ways of looking at things,
Let us, like travellers, be surprised on returning
To find the familiar strange, an otherness even
In our own homes – and be happy to find, at times,
As we look out of the window we thought was a picture,
That a leaf is part of a table; the plain sky,
Simple heaven; a stone, always a stone.

The Dart Estuary: Whitsunday

What light could be more generous than this?
A million multiples of here and now
Tingle on the face of the water, kiss after kiss.

For hours, from high on a hill, came the crackling morse
Of guns, where tiny marksmen lobbed clay disks
Up into blue, by a vivid crescent of gorse.

Lower, a steam train passed, squirting smoke in plumes
Out through steep trees. To the west, a naval band
Wrestled with a tune that wobbled in the wind's volume.

Now, near evening, the lavish boats
Nod to the last of themselves. Along the shore,
In oil-green shadows, a hazy stillness floats.

The silence hums, a treasure-house of each
Glint of sound, where all the colours melt
To gold and then to blankness, uncoined speech.

Mast-high already, springing clear above,
The wafery moon swells to its own calm gloss,
Subsuming every language under love.

The Artist at 81

Plain truth has become his only ornament,
Beguilement, first nature. With one white handkerchief
He will conjure the real world! Each hydra hand
Will meet the span required.

His repertoire goes down like a favourite meal:
His mind and heart savour the exact weight
Of all the notes, as one by one they ripen
Each in its own tempo.

It does not surprise him that the audience weeps:
Long ago, tears were the motherland
Of all his craft, twins to the blinding gems
Pinned to a tyrant's chest.

In this, his fine economy of age,
Nothing is show. Simply his music spells
A fluency of blessing to drown out
The worst of history. He need not even look
To know that we are weeping.

FROM **AQUAMARINE**
(1988)

Out of Land

Contained in this expansive privacy,
The hull nudged by tides, the world appears
Secure as the bleached decking, the halyards coiled
And cleated at the mast. For sure, morale
Arranges itself as simply as light and shade...
Until, on some unknowable day, there comes
A notion of land, that old affinity.

At first, a mere perversity of the water –
The swift run in, the luscious soft embrace,
A squirt into rich dark coves, a dusting of air
Where spray flings finely up from rock and blow-hole.
By logical extension, then, the trees
Arcing across the sparkling sand – the bay,
The gaudy parakeets, the trapped lagoon.

And soon the exile's fervent civics stem
All rainstorms. When the sea-fret clears the bay
It leaves, spick in bright sun, a noble polis
Whose hundred towers all speak a single language –
Whose sons, it will be said, shall never dream
Disloyalty, but whose pale eyes already
Reflect the tumbling deserts of the sea.

Rain at Sea

It rings the raddled waves, pocking
The long troughs with icy shot,
Replacing the horizon deftly
With its cold, sea-rain ghosts –

Of the captain pinned in the tall wheelhouse,
His pinched and bearded face that peers
Onto sheer disasters, the oncoming truth
Of irrefutable, house-high crests;

Of the green cabin-boy, so pale
And pretty, felled by sea fever,
Tipped from under the ensign, in the lee
Of the Horn, the crew on deck, grim-faced;

Of the ship that steers through every weather,
Doubling the Cape of Immoderate Hope,
Wheel lashed, bound for the shores of
Dark Narragonia, Never-Never...

The rain, the seething rain that falls
Knows more of soft corruption than any
Churning depth. The sea's decks,
Awash, grow wormy as any wreck.

The Bell-Buoy

Out past the cliff's redoubts
And the listing deck of the beach
Where the smart winds abduct
Our evolved words, it is hardly
The waves that stir, you'd say,
But something hidden under
That flexes, swells, slurs,
Scuds and trawls – the surface
Being only appearance
Like that thick lacqueur of sunlight
That floods the faring sea –

So with the bell-buoy, although
It remarks itself with drapes
Of weed and gaudy rust
And, in its iron ribs,
With the beat of the breathing bell
Jauntily syncopating
The undertow – yet it stands
For something else, unseen,
The sunken risks that are
Inimical to landfall:
Its only help is warning.

For lolling trippers' boats
It witnesses the point
Of turning back, at which
The heart grows calm again,
The land larger. But once
In a blue moon, in a flat
Calm, there is nothing but
A basking silence, the base
Of the buoy slowly turning –
And the questions come: what
Is absent? What is this warning?

Calm Sea at Night

Darkness instinct with life
Where beacons wink like cats –
Below the horizon they seem
Soft as torchlight shone
Through skin: diffuse, precious.

Love, it must be, or at least
Seduction – the trailing trills
Of phosphorescence glinting
In the water's wicked chuckles
As it collapses into whirlpools.

Tender on the face, the wind
Blows steadily, a pressure
To be trusted, a clean whistle
Of salt, entirely innocent
Of the earth's night-time coldness.

Each masthead light parades
Its triumph of pride across
The viscous, quickening sea
Where all engines turn
In a self-forgetting sleep:

And the moon, when at last it breaks
Free from the trawling clouds
Can do nothing, pale and swollen
As it is, but carry over
Our dreams to the coming dawn.

Wreath

Down from the steep grey decks it falls,
A gaudy lifebelt banging flat onto
Small waves, the fragrant fifth
Of a sonnet, *O bleu* that the blue ocean haunts.

Dying, already the leaves are curling,
Pitted with acid: the sweet-smelling cram
Of lilies and roses sucks at salt
And rust blooms at the wire's bright core.

Until, miles from land, the bees
Home to sip this sweetness which
For a moment stems the long tides –
Honey salvaged from the darkest sea.

Small Island

Always the sea at the end
Of the lifting corn, saying
Here is the gift and the gift's
Containment... And the firm arm
Round your shoulder of the harbour
Wall, saying that here
Experience and meaning are one.

All that is said is a kind
Of concession, a clause mortal
And strong as a sudden pool
Of sand discovered right
At the heart of the desert's blue –
A swirl of oystershell seen
In a bird's-eye view of the possible.

Anchor

Hope plucked
From the misty mud,
All its paid out
Scope is hauled
To the bitter end.

A blessing, an icon,
It rises to light
Through bubbled pressures
And the fish flat
As pressed flowers.

Firstling of
The imagination,
Already it drifts
Free beneath
The boat going on.

Great grey hook,
Even when landed
On deck it keeps
The look of clear,
Ancient depths.

Lastage of
The imagination,
Chained to the live
Hull of history
It holds fast.

Harbour

We have died and died into this new life,
Made peace with all the houses which we left
And long since said farewell to the *avant-garde*
Of new horizons, as to the *arrière-pensées*
Of numberless prodigal dreams...And now there is
The light leaping from water to flick across
The paintwork of houses and hulls, the unspoilt warmth
Of immediate sunlight baptising us into age.

The smell of fresh bread carries over the water.
Churchbells, laughter from pubs, the mail – small treats.
And even if nothing has quite the depth that once
We expected, here all the tides rock back to balance.
Over the cocktails, almost we could envisage
Accepting this, our fondest image of death.

Old Man Dying
(in memory of Patrick Campbell)

The whole bay, like a rich skin
Puckers at his touch, dips like silk
As huge, at home, he wades in.

I know it cannot be quite true –
He is not here, but on the hill,
Counting for safety to see him through

Dying – but here, his premature ghost
Baptises itself, mastering death
On a gentle Lilliputian coast.

An old man who dips and wades
Past the hour of his mortal strength,
Back bent now, the body splayed...

And at the side of the cot, his hand
Lifts. The water folds across.
Unseen, perhaps he steps onto dry land.

FROM **OUT OF LAND**
(1992)

Proofs

Delete leaves, the hum of long evenings, light.
Change to bold the grip of frost, black nights.
Rearrange forest gales, seas steep as stairs.
Italicise the stinging slopes of rain.
Stet the murderous world, heartland of despair.
Indent: in the beginning, begin again.

Insert an asterisk over Bethlehem.
Replace damaged characters with wise men.
Substitute stable for inn, manger for bed.
Transpose caviar and crust, fish and hook.
Realign hope, cherish the hungry and the dead.
Print: weigh in your hand spring's budding book.

Flight 000

It sags, the bright machine,
From level to level, swooping
Down beneath the canopy
Not of sky but forest.

Not clouds, but green boughs
Flick and snap at the windows,
Grazing the glass like rain
On through the avenue of trees.

And all this time, vainly,
The meticulous self-adjustments,
The throttling up and down,
The engines' whining obedience...

And this is the dream's substance –
Not the crash that must come,
Not the brute brunt in which
Limbs are a scattered luggage –

But this: the silver body
Perfect, graciously tilting
Along the narrowing flightpath,
Its illusory odyssey.

Recurrent

The rocking-horse stands in the hall:
You want to ride it and when you do
Your parents ride away from you.

The matron here is very tall
And creaks a little. Though she's trim
Her mouth is tight and rather grim.

The voice is shrill but when she tries
To charm you – *Just drink up your milk* –
It goes all smooth and soft like silk.

When you arrive you want to ride
The rocking-horse. You have to queue:
That of course is how they get you.

Barred gate, small trees along a drive
That dips, then rises. Your mind won't let
This image fade, or you forget.

They cure the children's nightmares – *Only
A week or two, it won't take long* –
But what child can tell the time of wrong?

The rocking-horse is never lonely –
You ride it every night and then
Your parents ride away again.

The Ravaged Place

(after Klee)

A mad skewed cone of ice,
A dunce-roof of disgrace:
It is here you told a lie
And could not show your face.

At night the air constructs
Raw blue and green around it:
You have never seen this place,
Yet long ago you found it.

The windows suck and suck
The light away. The door
Is silted up with dark:
Darkness on every floor.

It cuffs the sky, a tower
Of shrunken hurt whose name
Is that of a child gone missing
In a landscape of wobbly games.

The black wind here will blow
For ever, and each cross mark
What might have been before
The ice came down in the dark.

Early Service

Seen from behind, billowed and billowed
By his working elbows, after the blessing,
The priest's fine surplice was hardly credible –
All that washing and drying of silver,
Such energy of cotton, of elbows. And the clang
Of the paten and chalice seemed almost to ring
Untrue: as much an admission of wrong
As the view to be had at the altar rail
Of grey flannel trousers beneath the cassock
And perfectly ordinary secular shoes.

It was all secrets, a peek-a-boo glimpse
Between fingers, as the priest and server
Cruised past, crunching the dust like sugar.
And nobody knew at all what it came to,
That final huddle in the vestry after
The prayer they whispered: that conspiracy of counting.
How many coins stacked up into Babels?
How many sweets or buttons discarded?
They worked in the yellowest possible light.
Outside, dawn warded the winter darkness.

Skull

Helmet of bone
Bronzed with lichens,
The art of the possible
Seems still to hide
In your dark sockets,
The gone nosepiece.

Superfluous, you guard
The voided citadel:
Long ago they left,
Those sly defenders
Whose best form
Was always attack.

What matters now
Is quite beyond
Your scuttled casing,
Lodged already
In other minds
Or buried in books:

Even, perhaps,
Such deathless words as
I'll love you, always,
Though *Faugh! Faugh!*
Is the sound of the wind
In your imperfect jaw.

Mandelstam's Bundle

The word is a bundle and meaning sticks out of it in various directions
OSIP MANDELSTAM

In the direction
Of a tramp's belongings
The kerchief economy
Of common ground
The direction of hope

In the direction
Of vulnerable nerves
To be soothed and healed
At the least touch
The direction of love

In the direction
Of a mine's triggers
To explode in the face
Of a passing tyrant
The direction of justice

In the direction
Of the word's own authority –
Lictors of logos!
Binders of beauty!
The direction of truth

In the direction
Of names to be honoured
The one double meaning
Of Mandelstam
The direction of courage

Going Under

White, as you would think, but unkind –
A lack of grace. Nothing could prevent
The necessary needle from finding
Its mark. I remember, blurring behind,
A smile awry on a leaning face.

Chloroformed, flowers fold to sleep.
Smothering heat. Somewhere, a clatter
Much like the bang of a falling heap
Of pans. The canteen? Tinny, cheap.
Why, at that, does the heart miss a beat?

White, as you'd think – and the bed, the bed
Wheeled away now. It springs across
Joins and strips. Close to the head,
Children patting blankets. Leaden
Lids. Accepted – everything, anyhow.

Heroic Roses

The soft steel of moonlight never
Breaks through this forest. Only green
Plunders and narrows the dank air,
Only dark birds inch intently
Deep in its gathering rummage of growth.

But even here, so far beneath
The flickering patches of sky, at the verge
Where memory fades back to history and
The rose becomes the idea of the rose –

They are here, actual, heroic, the velvet
Of blood, their fragrance a giddying sweetness:
Whose thorns are sharp as steel, whose hearts,
Inviolate, are soft with what
They know of death and the far moon.

Chameleon Song

Against red – a robin, or Santa's sleeves,
A scatter of peppercorns on oiled green leaves,
Or the blood no grief retrieves;

Against yellow – starlight thick as yolk
Pouring past the hunched grey headstones, to soak
The grave no birth revokes;

Against brown – public as hope or dust,
Soft as a cow's eye, fine as hourglass rust,
Time that no heart can trust;

Against blue – the night's tall inky drapes,
The cursive blue of children's dreams, those shapes
No quick feet can escape;

Against all these, though hard to see, may move
The old chameleon, in air still crammed, above
God grounded, the hard rebirth of love.

Purple
(for Pauline Stainer)

It is the precise
Blur of the fact
Being more than itself –
The smudge of corolla
Which is not detached
And does not belong.

And what are those acts
Of purple penitence
And royal mourning
But the quickening heart
Of imagination
Bearing with loss?

You wear it as if
On principle, almost –
It will always be
(Even if only
An earring) somewhere
About you, like a clue.

Like the word discovered,
Like the beating image
Held steady, that may
Yet spill over
Its own border
Into true silence.

Priest Dreams
(for Erica)

Again and again they kiss the priest.
He is still silly with sleep and sits
Rubbing his eyes, like a tubby child.
Behind stained glass, the lights of candles
And joyous singing, where the smiling crowd
Collects its food, the body and blood.
A grinning cook tempts me to eat
A cream cake which I cannot afford.

In other dreams, I see him hunched
Like an old chesspiece in the darkened church:
And, over his shoulder, the glowing letters
Of the book at which he mildly gazes.
The tall gladioli which shoot at his side
Have the colour of apricots speckled with blood.

The Fish
(for John Halkes)

Deeper and slower the fish moves,
Each inch swum is gain of what
Already is sensed – the grain of each
Criss-crossing current, the rise and fall
Of every dot the ocean sieves
Nearer and nearer to nevermore.

Heavier, older, it cruises forward
Arrowing the tonnage of salt aside,
Letting the element work in its teeth –
Kyle of flesh, it flows between
Eternity and now, catching the light
Sometimes like sudden fire on its scales.

Perspective

Another Annunciation – the soft entreaty
Against a triptych of windows. But who could form
An angel from that black moth wildly beating
Behind the closed door?

No artist quite contains the landscapes locked
In these embrasures – the geraniums, not lilies
Spilling from the prosperous breastpockets
Of well-cut balconies;

Or, in the middle window, the path that winds
Towards the rosy castle – where in dead ground
Children must ignore the talking birds and find
Their way past slavering hounds;

Or the third – an arrowed brightness, heading through
Sunlight lost in shafts, past chiming cattle
High above the honed spire lapped in scales, to
The point at which, looking back,

You might see a true annunciation – the world
Innocent as an egg on public view,
Nested unbroken beneath the empyrean furls
Of Mary's immaculate blue.

By the Canal
(for Catriona)

She had done nothing wrong, but her guilt
Gleamed blackly on the slack surface

She had done nothing wrong, but her shame
Stood in judgement from the high poplars

She had done nothing wrong, but her tears
Stung her cheeks raw in the smoking sunlight

She had done nothing wrong, but her breath
Blurted and blurted in the drenching dew

She had done nothing wrong, but her mind
Could not escape from the jumbled hulk

Of the sunlight, the trees, the water,
The terrible guilt at the nothing she had done.

Driving Westward
(for my mother)

For Polesworth now read Holsworthy: on Radio Three,
Continuity, Dowland's sighing tears. Each tree
Wields its true flail, the Atlantic wind's corrective:
The rusts that gnaw the hedgerow look infective.
By Germansweek and Ashwater, low mist,

A scrim of green, the threadbare rain persisting,
The fields unleavened by light. Here and there,
A horse and rider draggling in the drenched air.
So it is that, driving towards the west,
I think of the poet's impulse towards the east
Which now the mirror shows as a grey and thin
Oblong where car-lights grow larger or diminish –
The occasional driver grimly making way
White-faced and frowning into the blinding spray.
To imagine the poet imagining God I find
A fine enough conceit, even a kind
Of consolation – as if, simply by driving
In the same direction on the same day could imply
An echo of faith, a journey back and on
Under a sky on fire with that long gone
Certainty. Now as then a poet must
Make the best of what is to hand and trust
To his luck lasting – and even en route to friends,
Remember to honour means as much as ends.
As if...I stare at the screen, its constantly blurring
Transparent Jackson Pollocks wiped off, recurring
(Frank O'Hara declared the artist to be
'Tortured with self-doubt, tormented by anxiety')
And try to focus on what there is to glean
From what there is, the collapsed cartography
Of faith's projections. And now my memory
Races ahead to where that western sea
Floods, ebbs and is steady beyond those hills
And valleys bright with kingcups, daffodils,
The blackthorn's small white stars – and there, one small
Boat is fishing, its blue hull rising, falling
Across the muscular swell...As if the weight
Of hills and oceans might be mediated
By one small flower, the merest bobbing ounce
Of fishhook fortune. Meanwhile, John Donne dismounts,
Keeping God at his back, content to know
The journey done, the poem safely stowed.

Paysages Moralisés

1

St George's eve – the elderly relatives brave
A cold April breeze, the twin uncertainties
Of pain and a world increasingly unbecoming.
But circling the Town Hall, by some swift magic we wave
Goodbye and cross a sunlit threshold into
The working model of a full-scale English spring.

Everything is impossibly in place –
The bluebell woods, their broad mauve-blue smudges
Never quite in focus, always bestowing
Too late, as we pass, a corporate vision of grace.
A mile on, the opening over of the village season,
The bowler lumbering up, unfit and blowing.

There is even a bride by the Thames, frilly and stiff,
Marooned for photos on a little island of grass,
Standing between two bridesmaids with bouquets.
Later, a hotel tea – and then we drift
Homewards, the car purring easily beneath
Aisles of blossom rocketing in high sprays.

Lost in the hollow acoustic of a dream, my mother
And aunt are borne along – beguiled, but no longer
Convinced by ancient emblems such as these.
Seeing, for one thing, the bowler's clenched fist: for another,
That bridal dress brittle as icing, as ready to snap
As the mantrap half hidden by the bluebells' tender leaves.

2

Grand high billows, Constable cloud
And, far beneath, an eyepiece made
From perfect hedgerows, arching trees.
Summer is a natural art, its peepshows
Aimed at infinity's parallel poles.

We look down on a hayfield pale
And razored as any in the quilted counties
Of southern England. Under the haze,
An atmospheric that the working gears
Of distant machines can hardly parse.

The car creaks as it cools. Lunch
Is exemplary, laid out inch by inch –
Fluted spring onions, carmine radishes,
Ham, lettuce, tomatoes, bread
And wine. The rug hugs the slope of the field.

The picnicker's art is deftly to fold
Past and future into the shape
Of now: in genuine hampers, to ship
The freight of leisure to the open air,
To remake Elysium from things as they are.

But try as we may, something has faltered.
No version of pastoral can filter
Justice from beauty: its silver tongue
Cannot hope to delay for long
The storm looming, the weight that has massed

Outside the frame and surely must
Burst any moment. We pack and drive straight
Back to the city. Beggars. The streets
Padlocked. Cardboard shelters. Time
Beating like a held bird, longing to fly.

On Remembrance Day
(for Charlie)

The golden rages of autumn,
Each immolated tree doused with sun
And set on fire

But not there, at the heart
Of the wood, in the weighty quiet withholding
Of its lumbered room

There, death can be followed
Precisely, its every step is tagged,
A shivering hawk-bell

The bell, then solid silence
Ringing in the ear. The drums of pheasant-feed
Leak one grain more

The bell, softly clacking,
And already waiting at the next silence,
Squeals of pain

Later, dark wings shrug
Upwards to settle calmly on the crown
Of a tree still in flames

Elements

It becomes in itself
A possessed medium –
The dripping musk-air
Of summer darkness,
The nervous window-frames
Clearing their throats –
Or withdraws to gesture,
Optative, flicking

A feather's hairs, then
Silent, an atmosphere
Passing through us
As it exercises,
As it bottles our words
In its wide bubble.

*

The footfall, for all
Its echo, must meet
The acoustic, dead
As adobe, which nothing
Can mitigate – pitiful
The bowls and bones
In the earth's hollows,
The earth which bears
All evidence of horror,
But that also gleams
With the springing wheat,
That barricades the sky's
Blank blue with green,
With the hopes of mortal love.

*

Paradox of flames –
Image of the flighty
Bird of hope,
But remorseless, the agent
Of mad moralities,
Requiring an exact
Rendering down
To the grey economy
Of ash: and too often
Infernal, that flickering
Brightness reflected
In our own eyes –
The books burning,
The phoenix itself consumed.

*

The world's shifting cargo,
Already it has crossed
The threshold to lap
At our little bones
With its wild choices –
To give or take
To buoy up or drown
To show or conceal
To bring home a cradle
Or the dark gliding boat –
It lies on our souls
Like an imprint of love,
Each moonstruck drop
Embracing the horizon.

Homage to Paul Klee
(for Pam)

1 *Alphabet Country*

And now you are entering
Alphabet country
You may look to lodge by the red road
In Villa R. The rates are reasonable,
The food adequate, instruction free.

In general, do not
Ask too many questions.
Y, by the way, is a gulf or bird,
Also the shapes of trees in a park
Near L (Lucerne is one suggestion).

You'll soon learn the logic
Of literal vision –
C, of course, for a ship in harbour,
H for father, thus I for mother,
While B gives birth to a composition.

Some meanings, though,
Can never be amended –
W is always woe, branded
On the child's brow: Mister Z,
Grim bossman, is hardly a friend.

Above all, beware
When letters attempt
To get together. Such combinations
Are IRR (quite mad) or RIP,
Perverse analysis (is that all it meant?).

The best you can hope for
Is a four-letter code.
Example: when L is not Lucerne
It could be Lily at the piano, playing
Bach in love's authentic mode.

Other examples:
Paul, or still better
Klee – a four-leafed German clover,
A French key and an English reminder
Of N on a headstone, the final dead letter.

2 *Tunisia 1914*

Over the harbour, the ascendant heat
Bleaches all colour. Tremulous palms
Cannot protect the wide sea
Or its last hope of blue. The curvature
Of the far horizon demands acceptance.
History looms like an old repeat.

Here in the blank and burning air
Daily the sun must realise
Its fierce liquidity. Even where
The mosque can scarcely maintain its streaming
Pillar of light, each glittering grain
Of dust is part of a call to prayer.

At dusk, slowly, the landmass cools
To colour. That angles sharpen to north
And south is as natural to you
As using the left hand for drawing, the right
For writing. Beyond the black minaret
A pale green moon makes beauty still seem true.

3 *Woodlouse*

When the sea goes down into its dark low cellar
And the restaurant on the Jungfrau freezes over,
There are still fish and birds to bear their witness
To silence and speech, to the deeply sunken sky
And the ocean overhead; to the innocence of colour.

The last year of your life. Again, here comes
The absurd and dangerous drummer who cannot bend
His knees. You feel your own membranes drying out,
Tensing you towards death. The desert cacti
Slide out from silos of shade to face the heat.

You find yourself in border country again.
The woodlouse, whose armature insists on blackness,
Is a skeleton fish, is the spine of a bird's feather.
Rolled up, it mimics a charred and hollow sun,
A black lifebelt in one corner of the sea.

It is a fossil of the will, of our little dipping
Into the elements for as long as humanly possible.
The way you have painted it, it might well be a last
Holy imprint, a springboard from which to leap
Clear to a world of silent birds, fish singing.

4 *Deep in the Forest*

Beyond the shade, beyond thought,
Beyond the very thought of shade,
The green heart of the forest hums,
An intensity immune to time –
Not to be weighed or measured, though
It is the power-house, the source.

The womb, the house, the garden gate,
The flower-lined path, all led you straight
Across the meadow into the wood
In whose dark ranks dark silence stood.

Here all invitations to meaning
Are elegiac in their outline,
Although provisionally you may call
This whirling mill a dim propeller,
This microphone a sunflower head,
This falling bird a wind-loose leaf.

You stood, then heard a distant stream
And ran to find it, ran till it seemed
Your heart would burst: then stopped. All round,
The sweet thick darkness, but not a sound.

How it swells and shifts and grows,
That green intensity of dreaming,
That sighing sea at the forest's heart –
And the little adult words drift down
And down, to break open and lie
Like pale casings on the hot floor.

Not a sound until there came
Those frightened voices calling your name.
You shivered with pleasure as you went on
Into the dark where you had never gone.

Departures

Set in a floral arcade,
These are the dreams of departures, in which
The ancient climbing roses are always
In bloom beneath the shivering glass
Of the station's forcing-house. Although
Figures must dwindle and twined fingers
Have to unclasp, the backward look
Stays for ever. On cheeks high-toned
With grief, a single frozen tear.

But dreams are dreams – already
The first bend has removed the station
From view, and the shapely words of thanks
And farewell no longer make sense as the engine
Rattles through landscapes to which they belong
Not at all. Accept, nonetheless,
This real ghost train of gratitude, of words
Marshalled before, to be printed after,
As the lights of the carriages shrink into darkness.

Last Rites

For two weeks now the old man has been trying
To peel the skin from his thumb, as if it were
A stall: but cannot. He works away at it for hours.

Meal-times bring other puzzles. His own hand
Mimics the hand that feeds him, tipping spoonfuls
Of thin-air soup into air, beside his mouth.

Nights are no better. Once, they found him stark
Naked and swearing loudly among the women
And had to hold him, drug him back to torpor.

Sometimes he calls for someone – a Mr Hogg,
Though no one knows him. Sometimes, he enquires
Whether his cases have been conveyed to the palace.

His visitors sit miserably, hoping
Time will go quickly – for him, for them. The lino
Gleams and gleams, harbouring no speck of dust.

At the Forest Edge

Between the low slate wall
And the green pagodas
The wood's breath passes,
Its palpable cool
A musk of sap,
A dark puff of knowledge.

Its lips might take you in
Beyond sunlight:
Beyond the first few
Visible yards
You would look back
To a pale strip of brightness.

Almost before you know,
On into darkness
Is the only possible
Path to take,
Away from a world
Scribbled across, erased.

Soon you will have forgotten
Even the gorse
That drifted over
The open heath,
Its exotic whiff
Of coconut and summer.

97

Wedding Song

(for Sophia and Robin)

Perhaps even here, among the airiest moments
Of wishing, there can be pre-emptive stillness –
As when the bride, gingerly easing out
Of the limousine, pauses, with barely a foot on the ground.

Or when the double-handed knife is poised
Above the hard and soft of the cake. When the pen
Inclines to its shadow, but the nap remains unscathed.
When the bell's clapper is still sounding the air.

Or when the vocative rings are still empty,
Held at the trembling tips of fingers that soon
Will almost eclipse them. When for a moment the light
Seems to thicken to a slanting smoke of dust.

And this, perhaps, is how love stows its gifts
Away, in little trices of silence. As when
The wind just curls away to nothing and even
The everyday waves of the lake are cured of time.

FROM **BUILDING INTO AIR**

(1995)

1

Three cities
would take several tellings
I laugh to myself

KENNETH WHITE,
Haiku of the Sud-Express

                    Across the square
Between the burnt-out Law Courts and Police Headquarters
Past the Cathedral far too damaged to repair,
Around the Grand Hotel patched up to hold reporters,
          Near huts of some Emergency Committee,
          The barbed wire runs through the abolished City.

W.H. AUDEN,
Memorial for the City

... that naked, hairless and eyeless horse that so many of
the survivors claimed to have seen in the ruined streets of
Hiroshima during the first days after the disaster. Its long
skull was encrusted with blood, for it was continually
colliding with the few walls and ruined houses that were
still standing; it would stumble on, wandering to the
irregular rhythm of its hoofbeats, now with flaring,
puffing nostrils, now with sunken head, now walking, now
mournfully trotting; on and on through the city as it
searched for a stable that was no longer there...

ROBERT JUNGK,
Children of the Ashes

Sketch

The city, which calls to mind
its own ignorance, its distance
from the waterfall that pours
over the lip of the hanging valley,
from the valley meadows packed with flowers,
from the great impervious beauty
of the high water cascading,
and the flowers that, countless, die.

Such will to order,
such unnatural power,
the night lit all through.

The Expedition

1

Early on, we dreamed
That we no longer had
A proper language, that
The punctuation had lost
All sense of order –
A breaker's yard
Of brackets, towering
Exclamations,
Stops running out
Into rank water...

2

When we turned away
To climb to the hinterland,
We could still hear
The inroading sea,
Its long scroll

Unfurling across
The glittering mica.
We listened to it almost
For longer than possible.

3

Basketwork, rafia
Bags or mats,
Oil-tins bent
Into mugs with handles,
Rabbits held out
In upturned hats,
Grubby salt-licks,
At night the sporadic
Kingdom of paraffin:
All of this
Was comprehensible.

4

Miles beyond
The backland's columns
Of jointed basalt,
Its wild escarpments
And cloud-choked forests,
There was said to be
Some crazed perfection
Of a capital, complete
With ten-lane boulevards,
Buildings as wide
As the open sea,
A bicycle to every
Thousand citizens.

5

One day we talked
Of home – the towns
Where shadow was perpetual,
With their little moon clocks,
Reliable markets
And the crackle of coal
In bellied iron grates.

6

Even the new coast
Has become articulate
In remembrance – the falling
Land clipped by salt
To the neatness of topiary;
The dusty square,
Its stoppered cannon
Thick with lacquer
And the stringy flagpole
Always ready
To salute a régime.

7

Almost the last
Words of our leader
Had to be heard
In the absurd context
Of whooping birds,
The gibber of monkeys,
The clicks and whistles
Of God knows what.
We have no authority,
He said – and the language
Simply came apart.

8

Tomorrow we press forward
To found a nation.

Before the Founding of the City

1

Bring pegs so as to mark out the place.
Bring two crowbars so as to dig post-holes.
There are no crowbars? All right then, sharpen two sticks.
Send out two men to the forest to cut forked pillars,
Two to look for strips of bark, and two more
To cut grass and others to look for posts.

2

The baboons have eaten all the peas and beans.
The clerk's daughter wants to buy some beads.
You have not yet paid your tax, what tribe are you?
If you want leave to be circumcised, I will sign
The registration certificate that you require.
All right, give me twenty-five cents, and I will give you
A stamp, some paper and an envelope.

3

Certain machines are distinguished by the sound they make.
Have you enough petrol to start the coffee pulper?
Is there any sim-sim oil for the thongs of the whips?
I shall plant fig trees to shade the coffee bushes.
The sun is strong, the stones are exceedingly hot.
The train has arrived. The almond trees are in fruit.
Bring me my photographs and that yard measure.
Tomorrow we build. I will write out your agreement.

(with acknowledgement to *Up-Country Swahili* 'for the soldier, settler,
miner, merchant, and their wives: and for all who deal with up-country
natives without interpreters': F. H. Le Breton, first edition 1936)

First City

In the first city I learn
the meaning of street level:
in the shadow of three faiths,
the shared belief in padlocks,
hasps, grilles, mesh,
nailed chipboard, iron bars.
And somewhere there is a window
locked solid with paper.

In the empty public gardens
the security men are talking
on their radios. Their bunches of keys,
heavy as a bull's balls,
weigh importance.

Beyond the undissenting suburbs
where the dentists surely live,
there is a road that goes on
for ever, where men in parked cars
are making anxious deals,
or failing to get in touch
with home on their mobile phones.

How the golden dome of the mosque
burnishes the sunlight to new!
And in the same sunlight,
near Limehouse Lock, a boy
and a girl are sliding through
a gap in the schedule of railings.

And who is that man petrified,
with his stone case to heel, outside
the station? It is hard enough
to live as any hero,
let alone the leader
of an expedition to Loughborough
undertaken for temperance.

Paddy (dear heaven, how he laughs
at the camouflage of his name!)
somehow must get across
three major roads, carrying
his bag of extra strong cider,
to the safety of the Red Cow.
He's OK, but his head
hurts where he was beaten up,
Christ it hurts, but he knows
enough to shake the hand
of whoever helps him get there.

By the main gate of the cemetery
it is all clearly typed out –
the distance the law requires
between bone and brick,
coffin and vault, neighbour
and neighbour, and cold earth.

And how shall the word
ever comprehend the flesh?
The word in acronyms,
the word in Gujarati,
the word in the underpass
where a man and his dog
express a single curse:
the flesh in the tonnage of dust,
the flesh in the piled markets,
the flesh in the growing gaps
that words leave between them.

Twelve oranges a pound
twelve juicy oranges there a pound
twelve oranges in a carrier bag
twelve juicy oranges in a carrier bag
twelve juicy oranges there in a carrier bag.

And who is that impresario
of the wholesale hangar, researching
the great cauliflower scam,
his thin mouth barely holding
a fat, cheap cheroot?

City of exquisite addictions,
your sweetshops split
each atom of taste
and confect each shape
to responsible living:
beyond the countless
emporiums of sarees
stitched and studded
a thousand times,
Ganesh looks
completely at home
in the bays of inland villas.

Two Views of the City

The first, optically false but true – the vertical,
the image of the thematic mapper sensor –
dear God, you think, and how could anyone live
in such a vascular wilderness, when the river
is already more black than blue, and seems to cringe
away from the land? And then, the land itself,
dyed into patterns of heat and bruised blue...

The second, horizontal – you squint across the roofs
to more walls and more roofs, and then more walls –
but everywhere, the windows march along
and up and down, sucking the poor day in.
The sunlight that strikes the occasional blank surface
is the last. If you wanted a proof of madness, you know
it is here, in the angles which finally cannot hold.

Second City

Someone must have read it
as a threat – the weight of civic pride,
the stupendous mass
of a reclining woman,
the four great stone lions
eroding to a sick pallor.

It is said that the moon
is never seen above this city,
and that each night a voice
proclaims the death of the lyric
in its dreamless streets: and, yes,
above the patchy darkness
diluted by orange,
the stars go by.

And it can seem that simple
when by ten at night
the deserted streets are dug
and drilled under arc-lights –
or at noon, when the city
stands back from the river
and all its tatty towers
shrink to perspectives of distance.
Or at any time, throughout the city,
when the brewery's absurd huntsman
begins to raise his glass
but never slakes his thirst.

You look like a gentleman.
I wouldn't be asking you otherwise.
Something for a sandwich.
I spent last night cold
and locked up into the bargain.
They said I was drunk but I wasn't.

The hospital, the library, the courts:
everything bloated, simply just too big,
tripping over itself, like the hillside
that has become an administrative
headquarters, its contours
mashed to tarmac access.

But the camouflage itself fails –
the brand names, the chain stores,
the *décors*, and the outdoor escalators
already bright with moss,
the church tower cobwebbed with cables
for fairy lights, by the flagpole
bandaged in saffron cloth:
even the poet attempting
to sneak past under the cover
of a top hat. Even the man
snapping the wipers off cars.

Everywhere, you suffer the weight
that throbs off the angles and acoustic
of water, that aches up through your feet
as you skirt the uncrossable carriageways;
that presses down through the tower blocks.

What changes hands down the long roads
out of the centre, is one or another
version of the rumoured velocity of escape.
In one palm, money; in another, money.
Between them, the trip, the wad shot. Yeah.

And everywhere, the bright attempt to build
the city's simulacrum into high air,
to roof in the clouds
or suspend a biplane from wires,
to construct terraces that give onto
pure layers, with thoroughfares
of wind and rain, balustrades
for sunlight to lean over.

Would-be arcades of amnesia
full of glitter! But what really shines
is the thought of heavy bulldozers, heaving
the lot – jewellery, crafts, crystal,
aromatic lotions, leather goods, watches,
finest knitwear and fancy breads –
over the edge, into the sea.
In the blue corner, those who believe
in aesthetics and stewardship:
in the red, the champions of
community and conscience.
Let all the world...

Between the clouds and the stone, there is
one green bottle, balanced on a wall,
half light, half full – and this:
the voice of its owner, from across the road,
as he leans into the gutter and wails,
For Chrissake, I'm only forty-seven!
(and the whole of the city seems to lie
refracted in the liquor's
bright, stilled horizontal)
Only forty-seven years of age!

An apparently endless silence,
a time-lapse sequence jammed
at a point where glass
refuses to crumble to sand
or fuse to rock:
and, in the Mandela Gardens,
where the tulips are in their cups,
nothing stirs to confirm or deny
his words locked into stone:
the struggle is my life.

The Authorities Attempt to Keep in Touch

Like, nobody wacks the rulers' tag,
since they are always fly and dope –
it's time to tell you our party's kicking.
This is nothing lame and nothing rank:
we want to be your homies, your crew.
We're no way sketch, our G. style's rad –
don't you go saying we're a ho
or that we're getting busy. Like,
we're O.G., you better check it out,
we're chill on slate, no hole in our bucket,
hot knife or bong or skinning up's
cool on any turf, we're tooled up,
we've got the juice, the decks and rags –
don't you step to us or say we're wiggers
or biscuit heads. We're stupid, the law,
we've got your G. style and your jewels,
we're on a trip and stoked. If you kick
off, we'll soon be painting black tears.
Like, nobody wacks the rulers' tag:
our homies, if you're cool, that's you.

Third City

Somewhere between
the two cathedrals
an unhurried sax
yawns the length
of a whole dark street,
plosive, then
huskily pulsing,
lax and lovable.

It could not be enough
to make for coherence,
though it conjures nostalgia,
the ghost of hope:
here, no gloss of renewal
can quite exorcise
the pale ships that nose
through early mists,
the buried lines,
the fairground rattle
of the airborne railway.

But what is more wrecked
than a stove-in roof?
What grass is tougher
than the roof-level tussocks?
What could be more on fire
than the roaring waste,
the rage of endless torching?
Here, the psalms
are true songs of anger.

At times like this
you would say, perhaps,
that the city was ill-founded
or gone to seed:
too many scumbled stones,
too much paintwork
all scab and crust;

too often exhibiting,
as with the wire
exoskeleton of the palm house,
a pathology beyond reason.
Too many ownerless dogs
that run towards you
at a menacing diagonal,
their large ears pricked up:
too many bottles lobbed
into hopeless areas.

It is nothing that time
cannot also cure.
Meanwhile, in one cathedral
crouches a secret brass mouse,
an antidote for children
to the gaunt scale of belief;
in the other, the archbishop
is pictured showing
a docker's hook
to Monsignor Furneval,
as if to say
that here too
the world is everything
that is the case.

In the mute shadows
of words, in the inches
of their worn columns,
somewhere there is hidden
the exposed life
of the actual city,
where the saxophone leaves
each phrase wide open
to interpretation
and the river's régime
goes on for ever.

Near Endings

Flayed by fire
the horse of Hiroshima
knocks its blind bone and blood
against brick, wood.

On another coast
the rain surges in swathes,
trees flip like tossed cabers,
even though the trams go on
dragging their rust and clank
on from prehistory.

To each city its bunting,
its brightness, its high tides,
its inflorescence of rusts,
its mechanisms of disaster,
the moment when all the little boxes
of livings, the ingenious tins,
are folded away or scattered.

And there comes to each
some laureate of lassitude,
a dark-eyed dandy
of love and war,
or a crusty slippered poet
with his carpetbag spilling
frayed, half-finished maps.
He takes his time,
shambling in the last of sunlight –
commissioned by himself
and pensioned off,
knowing it needs more
than geese to save a city now.
Compline shall be his swansong,
his chosen vanishing-point.

Yet even here,
long after the horse,
after heat that unlocked
the seeds as well as the stones,
the city has fruited
into strange newness –
has gone on to where
the long sickness
begins to look
like just slower forgetfulness,
the brutal inconsequence
of time passing.
Unless those hoofbeats
are not growing fainter
but louder, drumming
our haunted futures.

2

An Afternoon Walk

Your dog could swim for ever, it seems,
Along and back in the moorland river,
Exploiting his spaniel inheritance
As fluently as a swan.

We sit watching him bite the bubbles
At his own mouth. Above the softly
Buckling water, low cloud
Heats the glare.

As we go back, you throw a simple
Fistful of air for your dog to chase:
He will run for ever, it seems,
Suspending disbelief.

And somewhere in this lies a small quotient
Of sadness, which might be the number of times
That love goes into a lifetime,
Or the plain measure

Of another day played off against
The version of infinity still locked up
In the question I haven't asked
And your answer.

Seeing Through Water

Not so much when, on your back
Within the blue-green O of the pool
You lie there, calmly floating,
Open and exposed,
With only the thin lapping sheet
Between you and the sky,

But when you swim length after length
Widely stroking the flow aside,
Is when you seem most at risk,
Most precious – with your hair
Sleekly dark and combed back from your temples
By the water, as you part it.

It is something about the paleness of your brow,
Your head held just clear of the pool
And turned slightly to one side;
Your arms that meet
And spread, pulling the water back,
And close to meet again.

It could be a dream, the way in which
You come and go, crossing the criss-cross
Dimples of blank and blue,
But that the water
Magnifies, clear of all distortion,
A simple, shining truth.

Another Parting

Remember how we gunned the car down the motorway
Towards the airport's absurdly slow
Litanies of departure? – Check-in, the catechism
Of security questions, the electric angelus
Of chimes, passport control, the gate...

When, somehow, we managed to say
Goodbye, we felt we were being crushed
By the weight of time that had massed above us
Like the grey cloud into which you would go:
And, through it all, an orphan half-phrase
Rang in my head – but a mad contradiction
Of what was real – *Time that is given*...
Today, as another parting comes closer,
The words recur, along with that cloud
Which moves over each lived minute of love.

But today those minutes have all the brightness
Of your favourite gemstones – the steady burn
Of garnets, the amethyst's clear purple,
The mallow-green of malachite, with its swirl
Of black contours beneath the surface:
As if parting itself could just be
Like seeing sunlight pinch the ocean
Into points of sparkle, or like the way
In which now that phrase finds its sudden completion –
Time that is given has no shadow.

No shadow – simply the winking grains
Of all those minutes which fire and flare
Along the runways that lead into darkness:
And, beyond, the calm patterns of the stars,
The bearings which fix our new arrivals.

The Bruise

One night you ear-marked me,
Yet even when the bruise blossomed
In mauve and yellow on my arm
Where your head had rested, I failed
To recognise it as
The simple blurred imprint
Of the ear-stud you had worn.

But once you had explained it,
I wore that mark with the pride
Of one on whose poor flesh
Appear the stigmata of a love
Which, even after the cloud
Of old blood has paled,
Still lasts and lasts.

Sweet Chestnuts

Not to name the object, but to display
The sweet chestnuts, conceivably becomes
A homage to the simple quiddities –
For instance, how on the drenched October grass
They lie splayed out, their quilled green mace-heads utterly
Exploded to reveal the hair-soft linings
Of not quite yellow, not quite white or grey:
And, oddly square, the tenements of brown fruit,
The three or four that stand up at the centre,
Loosely socketed, easily dislodged.

There comes the sense of something secret shown,
Of some exposure tender to the touch,
An inkling offered of what it is that denies
The object its loneliness, its independence.
Above the fallen fruit, the swelling tree;
Below, the twisting contexts of the roots.
Within the object, unnamed, the hidden subject,
Its absence that homes to you as naturally
As the heart leaps at the single name of its love.

South Street Nocturne

The curtains breathe in and out
To the night wind, and the door
Of the tall cupboard sags open:
It would really be no surprise
If the drawers of the dressing-table
Slid open one by one.

Everything's joining in –
The dressing-gown hunched on its hook,
The louche bedside light,
Its shade pushed back from the heat
At an angle, the alternating hiss
And hiatus of a distant train –

Even the two of us, lying
Beneath the long cord
Of the light-switch that trails
To its plastic toggle; one
Of us asleep, and one,
Apparently, not quite.

Close to the bed, a clock
That seems to slow at each
Flick of a second, as if
None of this could be
(And could it?) more than a set
Piece of indolence, or love.

Ideogram

The way you write the figure 2
Seems purely anecdotal –
A love of narrative overcoming
The simple fact of a total.

You start by sketching a river surface,
A gleaming baseline of ink
That flows from left to right beside
The margin's vertical brink.

Then, rising against the current,
The elegant hook you draw
Is a fine swan's neck, rounding to dip
Down to the water once more.

You do it at speed, as if by sleight
Of hand, but still it displays
A figurative meaning more
Than sense alone conveys:

The sum of love as two-in-one
And more than either one could make –
The whole story of the river rewritten
Victoriously in the swan's wake.

Coming Down

In these scales, nothing
Is properly weighed –
Yet it is here
That you feel the machine
Feeling the full
Weight of its weight,
Each muscle of metal
As tested and stressed
As an old kneecap,
As the plane jags down
The staircase of air.

And for ever, until
The landing, it seems
That the land runs on
And on, below:
Lower, lower –
To the speeding cornfields,
The flicking hyphens,
Down through the airlock
Of absolutes, to the heart
With its balancing feather; to you
Waiting, on the light earth.

3

Sublunary

The moon's second reflection,
As it drifts into the depths
Of summer fields and turns us
To ghosts in our own landscapes,
Is the image of its ambitions –
To send the river rattling
Off on its stones; to outstare
The crop-eared owl; to reach
Right down to the dust
Of the tight avenues of wheat
And draw out from the earth
The monthly fullness of silence.

Prelude

Something is not being said,
But waited for all the same;
A train, perhaps,
Or a revolution,
Or an unjust king with a sword.

But the rim of a halo
Is understood, the current of air
From a bright wing flexing:
And somewhere a choir
Is floating its precise dictions
Calmly, beyond the announced silence.

Umbrian Song

(for Jimmy and Margie Campbell)

You have come to a landscape of transformations
Where hoses project white feather after feather
Across the maize, and every sunset
Is a Japanese flag flying close alongside
The flank of a Japanese volcano.

Locked in its dull tent, the caterpillar
Changes in private: but the scorpion crossing
The whitewashed wall is caught halfway
Between its lobster imitation and being
A sleek black galley with a high prow.

The breeze and the poplar, a double act,
Exactly merge to a full river's trickle –
And even time is no more, here,
Than a single laryngitic cockerel
And random churchbells tuned to no hour.

As for the sunflowers, they droop and droop,
Field on field of blackening shower-heads...
Meanwhile you sweat and sweep and scrape
And paint like fury, stubbornly shaping
The labour of love to a real house.

Fish Magic

Here lies the holy fish: its fading gloss
Comes off as tacky sequins on your hand.
Nothing averts its eyes of milk and glass,
Or improves the dead sourness
Of its downturned mouth.

White meat conveyed to the white tooth,
That melts in a memory of salt,
That leaves its last taste on your tongue –
But it leaps to life in a thousand
Chevrons of bone, is away
In infinite flicks of muscle,
In the only afterlife it knows,
The resurrection of numbers.

The Fullness of Glory

What narrative can move the silence on,
What silence appropriate the cries
Of those abandoned day after day by any
Hope of simple justice or of mercy?

It is more than our curiosity
Which betrays us. Yesterday, how peacefully
The stars shone! And any fruit, cut open,
Models the pure cosmology of perfection.

Propped on the Easter altar, the book still trails
Its markers of gold fire, imperial purple,
Dark crimson. Each week, from its spread pages,
Is read *Heaven and earth are full of Thy glory.*

The contexts accrue – another starving child
Hunching over the wreck of its own poor bones;
And, after stories censored by curt gunfire,
Accusations that hang like smoke in the silence.

Songs of the Darkness

In the buried darkness
Voices are welling
That sing and pray
In a language almost
To be understood.

In the painted darkness
The magi ride onward
With their blazing retinues,
Ignoring the huntsman
Who aches for blood.

In the darkness outside,
The leprous cities
And lush fields
Embody the world
In its broken beauty.

In songs of the darkness
The flowers of the dead
Are always in bloom,
And the birth of Christ
Is God's first wound.

Yet out of the darkness
Come such simple offerings
As ghee, fou-fou
Or maize, gifts made kingly
By the recognition of love.

Father to Son

(for Matthew)

No one would know, unless they actually knew –
Or even notice the drab brown building facing
The Apollo supermarket. Once inside,
Traffic noise or the odd branch waving from
Beyond the window are insufficient distractions
From evidence which multiplies in folders,
Time that aches and aches in clinic queues
And the outraged screams of children.

Each time we go, my heart begins to sink
Almost as much as yours must – most of all
When we first glimpse, beyond a door, then confront
Those alien machines, grotesque or sleek,
Whose circuits you, their missing part, must complete.
With all their tubes, dials, monitors and screens,
We have to trust them as benign, despite
The pain they may also bring.

Beyond all this – the caring smiles and skills
Of nurses and radiographers, and the doctors
So famous that, jet-lagged, they have to ring
In from the airport to give the go-ahead
For pre-meds; beyond the knowledge, too, that others
Are suffering more – a part of you still craves
A chance to reject it all.

And part of me, confounded by love and fear,
Would almost sign a pact as your accomplice –
Anything rather than more tinkering to cope
With a defect no one can help. Almost – forgive
That qualifying doubt whose other side
Is hope. Beyond a certain point of bruising
Neither can talk of this.

Fanfares at Eger

They appear on the hour, like figures
Geared to an antique clock,
Pinned on the narrow balcony
Of the town's thin minaret –
So high that you cannot make out
Their features, only admire
The last of the sunlight gleaming
On the bell of the wound horn,
The great golden paperclip
Of the trombone's slide, the valves
Of the two brilliant trumpets.

For half an hour exactly
They drive the birds crazy
With their rich party pieces –
Black as quavers, the swallows
Race through the pressured air,
Criss-crossing the flourishes,
The fanfares and the canzonas.
And, down below, a circle
Of pale faces peering, smiling;
And, inch by inch, the light going.

It could not reach out far,
This music, will never alight on
The still, green valley of Lídice,
Will not infiltrate
The huge, strutting concrete
Of Bucharest's leaky palace –
Yet even though, long ago,
The players bowed, turned and
Disappeared, the echo goes on.

FROM **THE WORLD RETURNING**

(2002)

Theatre Opening

Men must know, that in this theatre of man's life
it is reserved only for God and angels to be lookers on
FRANCIS BACON,
'Advancement of Learning'

This is the reservoir flooded to full
for the first time. It flows and wells,
its surface a restless glitter, its depths
already an unsounded spell.

This is the warehouse of ghosts which hoards
the poisoner's whispers, doomed queens and kings,
tramps in waiting and, beyond the wood
at Colonus, Œdipus fading.

This is where vowels imagine everything –
that wooden O, Poseidon's E,
upturned steel U, aluminium A,
I on a headland by the sea.

For this is state of the art darkness
in which the mind, all synaptic relays,
knows itself warded by true pretence,
a play within a play.

Everything here is absorbed on cue –
the belly laugh, the lethal kiss,
the armed silence, the unguarded look:
there is no end to this.

So begin. Bring on the hopeful lovers
with their young gestures, and the kindly clowns.
Here, as outside, only God and his angels
may claim to be lookers on.

1

The Pilots' Tea Dance

Everything at a slant:
the diagonal shiny boards,
the spotlight's smoky shaft,
the way they move the girls
held in their chevroned arms
to the sly foxtrot, the waltz;
and the camera that peers down
as if in search of hindsight.

Out of the sun, they wave
like the summer wheat outside,
lost in the only dream
that could hope to out-sing time
or the voice which knows that the field
is the world, and the reapers, angels.

The Musical Box
(for Catriona)

In the dark space under the basement stairs, it seemed
too big to be a casket. A child's coffin,
we sometimes thought, although it weighed a ton.
Never polished, it always gleamed and gleamed.

We hardly noticed, inside the lid, the display
of almost naked nymphs whose gauzy veils
wafted so decently. There were too many other things,
beneath an inner glass lid, to claim our attention:
the great rolling cylinder pimpled with tunes,
the double row of chimes and the strikers, each
stem topped with a little turban of brass;
the rabbit's ear of the lever which brought the strikers
to the bells or away; the great comb of metal
on which the music played. Best of all, the vane
that pirouetted on its spindle, its little paddles
easy to put a finger in and stop,
then let go again. Not to mention the tunes themselves,

twelve of them, every one prinked and decorated
with ornate arpeggios, *glissandi* bright as rain –
Can-can, Strauss, the Russian anthem, Brahms.

Squeezed in beside the box, sister and brother,
we might have been back in the womb – ghostly twins
hardly hearing the world, any more than the beat
of the flicking vane. Hardly knowing each other.

Painting of an Island

I dream of the prow with a bone in its teeth
and the foam squirting in two Welsh plumes,
the hull lifting, quivering like a fish,
falling with the thud of truth.

And astern, dwindling till it hardly rides
the swell, the mainland: ahead, somewhere,
the island hidden by the endless shimmers
that cross the spine of the tide.

It lies just over the strait. On Sundays
surely you could hear the bells, the prayers,
our Father – or laughter, from the houses
with verandahs and a view of the bay.

I know where it comes from, this little franchise
of biscuit-flat land crammed between towers,
with its church in a hidden square to which
the hidden streets must rise.

And I know how those two open boats on the quay,
one careened like an Auden slipper,
will always suggest the ease of crossing
and how it will always be

as out of reach, that island, as the parent
who sent his paintings for the children's rooms –
whose memory, over the years, became
ruinous with absence.

Black in the Early 1950s

For a start, the bags under Edgar Lustgarten's eyes
as he shook his jowls morosely towards the stalls
from his leather chair, a coal fire licking behind him –
Of all the cases that baffled Scotland Yard
surely none was more strange than that of the headless
body at Midhurst Station, one bleak winter night...

And then the film itself, in which an ambulance,
black, top-heavy, with great silver hinges,
would career down the curvy drive of a private clinic
in which some unspeakable procedure would be performed
without anaesthetic. Only the imagination,
wincing, could get past the doors with their blind port-holes.

In real life, it could be just as bad – a man
wrapped in red blankets and held in place with straps,
carried from a house in the street. Not a good colour.
The ambulance gleaming like a hearse, the silver trolley
shiny as a fish. We children gawped. They slid him
in on runners and shut him into the dark.

Back at the clinic, at the very moment when
the eyes above the mask narrowed, pitiless, and the hand
moved to make the incision, more sugar-crunching
of wheels on gravel – enter two black Wolseleys
with alarms clanging, rocking on their springs as out
leapt squads of policemen, all in their smartest black.

In 1952, a month or so before Newcastle
won the Cup for the second year running, black went
ballistic. Even the wireless rigged up at school
had its square face wimpled in black cotton
for The Funeral. Voices were solemn, close to tears.
One boy fainted. The teachers wore black ties.

Looking back, though, it's clear that really nothing
we saw at the Gaumont, the Odeon or the Savoy,
or in the street, or heard on the wireless at school
could hope to outdo the black of the late forties –
the aftermath of war, the cat slinking
across the dazzling dark toecaps of Harry Lime's shoes.

The Addiction

All this came late, as seemed to befit a house
with no father, where taboos had a low threshold –
you could make do with a sniff at an empty beer-bottle,
a lick of its black nubbed stopper; or with a quick
glimpse of the pub when the frosted door swung open,
the waft of talk and smoke yeastily there
and gone again. Once, a bottle of rum
with a top you flipped up, and the strange smell of dunder.

The litany of brands could well have been
a sufficient lure – Craven 'A', Abdullah,
Woodbines, Capstan Full Strength, Senior Service,
Player's Navy Cut, Du Maurier, Three Castles,
Gold Flake, Gitanes, Gold Leaf, even the absurd
exotic Balkan Sobranies with their gold-tipped black,
and the ones in soft packs closed with a paper seal:
Lucky Strike, Disques Bleus, Camels, Chesterfield.

Then, the procedures: the opening of the little drawer,
the whoosh, soft as satin, when you whisked away
the gold or silver foil, to expose them ranged
in perfect order, close and regular
as boxed eggs. Or, breaking the seal,
you gave that one authoritative tap
which brought out two or three just so far,
stacked like organ pipes, ready to offer.

After that, timing and expression were everything:
the flick of fire, the head inclined and then
tossed back, the lips and cheeks closed in on
the searing circle, the arc of the hand, the cool
considered exhalation and the look
that went with it. Whole systems could be stubbed
out, arguments clinched, an ache in the heart
be noble, or a hot affair be started.

It took another twenty years to learn
that real addiction might be something else –
the world returning, hyper-real enough
to drag your eyes from their sockets, and the size
of every leaf outsize, each object swollen
with its own savour and abundance. Even to enjoy,
when it was safe, the whiff of cedar and, slightly,
of caporal in the box with no cigarettes.

In Outline Only

As for the bedroom walls, three were already
full – the good old Kodak always did
the trick. Amazing, how at that age they loved
to pose. He focused them upright or horizontal
in the viewfinder's shining cross, flirtatious creatures!
Still room for more, though: the possibilities seemed endless.

                          *

Here was another twelve year old (or was he
only eleven then?) laughing, sucking on a pipe:
and there, a boy standing up through the sun-roof, waving.
Happy days. In this one, someone was trying
to light a fire outside a two-man tent.

                          *

He gave them presents and meant them. He also liked
the feel of flesh – to deliver a hard smack
and then let his hand stay clamped to the buttocks.
He regularly felt the need to pray.

                          *

He teased them with things they could not possibly know,
though he himself was puzzled by the way
in which one friendship ended, and another
soon began. They just did, it seemed.

*

As for the bedroom, impossible to tell
which of the pics were trophies, which (if any)
temptation withstood – and whether it was guilt
or simple prudence which made him strip the walls
bare one day, get rid of everything.

*

His later holidays were spent discreetly
in Bangkok or the Philippines. At home,
something that was not love but knew its gestures
ghosted the paler patches on the walls –
in outline only mirroring the stain
of hard facts spreading out through all those lives.

Fives Courts
(for Matthew)

In every place the courts were set apart,
hidden behind the armoury or the bike sheds,
a good place for a quick grope or a gasper.
Empty, they seemed banal as a torturer's cellar:
a row of sties that didn't smell quite right.

Blank walls, a toy door, four large lights
in metal shades with grilles, shining onto
slabbed stone. Along the front, a bar
of wood. In autumn, the courts streamed with wet:
in winter, the wind drove snow across the thresholds.

In an old biscuit tin, a selection of gloves
limp as exhausted fish; Slazengers, the colour
of dried blood, Grasshoppers a dull grey.
In most, the fingers unstitched, the padding lumpy:
in all, an ingrained smell of stale sweat.

Only the ball was intricate. On old ones,
like mad surgery, little spiralling lines
of red stitches pulled the cover tight
around a core of rubber, cotton and cork.
Nowadays they just glue the seams into place.

The play's the thing, pure ingenuity –
the crack of a service rocketing out from the corner,
the ball hammered off the back wall, the sly lob,
the boast that ricochets madly off one or both
side-walls and dies irretrievably by the bar.

Enter the ghost of Hazlitt, himself a player,
who wrote that 'poetry puts a spirit of life
and motion into the universe' – and knew
how much depended on the playful imagination,
on keeping warm in the coldest places on earth.

Not Admitting It

Your world worked almost perfectly: in your cellar
the beer ticked and fizzed. On your allotment,
year after year the scarlet beans raced up
the crossed poles, onions swelled their copper domes,
raspberries delivered their soft drupels by the score.

You had the world's number, knew to avoid
redcaps, rozzers, all agents of the state.
During the war, you heated your steak and kidney
on a tank engine's cover. In peacetime, drove too fast
(your wife knitting like fury) but spotted all speed traps.

Perfectly at ease, you went about trailing
a tea-cloth and duster, one from each trouser pocket.
Your moustache came and went – the pipe as well,
which took its turn with hand-rolled Rizlas so thin
they almost went up in the lighter's flame completely.

Confident, too – God knows what you smuggled out,
wrapped in brown paper, from the college buttery, certain
that somebody's blind eye was turned. And proud of your fitness,
bracing your stomach muscles, then inviting
a punch: *Go on, have another go! Harder!*

Your stories, like your laughter, described a place
in which, if you kept your wits, and one step ahead,
anything was possible. Scouting the world as it was,
you tutored us to share your love of jokes,
to see that defeat was the biggest joke of all.

Even at the end, when you lay all huddled up
in a hospital bed, you couldn't admit it, but just
yawned hugely, your tongue wagging mute in the middle.
All I could do was say *Take it easy, George*
and turn away: I knew you had gone already.

For Tony Lambert

Last night, hearing of your death at fifty-two,
I scanned the college photo of sixty-three,
willing you not to be there, among the rows
of the peaked-too-soon, the yet-to-become, the just right
pipe-smoking Tories, brilliant historians,
inscrutable civil servants of the future,
union officials, doctors, publishers, priests –
there, reliably, you weren't. And perhaps it is
that consistency of absence which makes it now
not just simple, but an imperative
to run to words so soon, somehow to track
that real and timeless ground which lies beyond
the real immediacies of grief and anger.

143

For time was never in it, not even in
the pendulum of the weighty grey and yellow
iron pan you gave me for my wedding,
though thirty years on it still makes wicked omelettes.
Somewhere I have a picture of you holding it,
in the front quad, on the day. Your smile. Your wide
eyes, a little heavy. Your relaxed stance –
everything conveying the flair I loved
and feared a little, because it seemed to offer
no guarantee of anything but itself,
and sometimes came too close to undermining
that notional justice which, I naively hoped,
might somehow still secure the world ahead.

Somewhere. Sometimes. Somehow. More recently,
we talked of meeting again, although our voices
down the line could hardly disturb the old
continuity of silence. And now, only this
monologue – but held clear of circumstance,
in a way that I think you would find funny, but also
understand. Your last plans, I hear,
included poems and an art gallery. I can offer
no other presence than this, along with the image
which I found today, on waking, in my head –
of a burnished fruit turning calmly on its branch:
perfect, beyond the reach of any trespass,
remote as the moon and radical as love.

2

Alfred Wallis's Vision

He saw how the land broke
on the shores of the sea,
how the ocean took on the colours
of the earth, and behind the lighthouse
whose tip seeded the dark
with winking brightness, there was nothing
but dead children.

For the grey sea laid claim
to everything as it shot
up over the shuddering deck,
the waves racing aloft
to soak the grey sails
and muffle the sky in a shawl
of grey salt.

And what was the land worth
but rag-and-bone,
birds in their fidgety kingdoms,
a few red-leafed trees
on a hillside, tiny houses?
And hymns played much too feebly
on an old melodeon.

Under everything lay
nothing from books
or London, but the huge fish
deaf to the world, gliding
on in their languid smoothness,
intent, slower than any
collapsing wave.

Staring at the boats heeled over
in the blue roads of St Ives,
the luggers, schooners, cutters
all alive in the wind and tide,
he saw that *each boat of that fleet*
had a soul, a beautiful soul
shaped like a fish.

A Flourish

(for Jimmy)

What if it were not at all
as painters once thought, the resurrection –
no marble lids flipped up, no smart
unsurprised bodies somehow jerked
back to the vertical?

Suppose it instead an abandonment, almost
casual, in springtime, all the cars
left on the sunlit roads, their doors
wide as open wingcases, engines
quietly ghosting.

Their owners having simply drifted over
to the cowslip kingdom of undropped keys,
into meadows where they kneel at flowers,
or beechwoods where they stroll across thresholds
of light and cover.

Here the orchid rises from the cross,
spilling droplets of blood from its stem,
and beneath the trees unlettered bluebells
wash onwards for ever, leaving the eye
at an utter loss.

Everything merges here – A and O
are as one, from Ophelia's early purples
to Ariel happily listening for owls;
and the little fritillary's chequered shade
is pure art nouveau.

And God? Would hardly, perhaps, believe
how simple his own life had become
on the far side of the trumpets, having
only to budget for continuance and devise
new sports and variations on love.

The Cablecar

The silver box rose lightly up from the valley,
ape-easy, hanging on by its one arm;
in minutes, it had shrunk the town to a diagram,
the leaping river to a sluggish leat of kaolin,
the fletched forests to points it overrode.
It had you in its web of counterweights,
of circles evolved to parallel straight lines.

Riding the long slurs, it whisked you over
the moraine's hopeless rubble. It had your heart
in your mouth at every pylon, where it sagged,
leaned back, swooped on. It had you hear how ice
cracked on the cable. It had you watch it throw
an already crumpled shadow of bent steel
onto the seracs. It made you think of falling.

By the time it lowered you back to the spread valley,
to the broad-roofed houses decorated with lights,
you could think only of what it was like to step
out, at the top, onto the giddy edge
of snowfields still unprinted, that pure blaze;
to be robbed of your breath by the thin air, by a glimpse
of the moon's daytime ghost on solid blue.

As When

(for Doctor Virendra Bhandari)

As when you gingerly open prayerful hands
to see what you have caught, that has been tickling
your palms with wings or feelers, and you find
only the thought of something bright and precise,
that must have somehow zig-zagged back to the sky,
its image too soon blurred to an idea.

As when, now, I try to recall the delicate
pink of the water hyacinths in Orissa,
the sweep of the beach at Puri, brown beneath
a haze in which stood huge sand-clogged propellers,
or the face of the modest doctor at Udaipur,
or the Konarak boys who wanted their picture taken.

As when they soar, the colonizing words,
up past the rattling crow trapped in the rafters
of San Thomé cathedral, past the pink hives,
humming with breezes, of Jaipur's great façade,
up to the vultures circling Golconda, to claim
a bird's-eye view beyond all contradiction.

As when MacNeice at Sheikhupura, finding
a massacre, did what he could to help the survivors,
but must have had to face again the shadow
that, dark as Durga, stalks his poems, an avatar
of absence cold as the stillness which comes with starlight
to haunt the high hot courts of Fatehpur Sikri.

As when, at evening, gently the descending plane
inclines its wingtip towards the thin blue cloud
that drifts over the city, bringing you back
to what is real, the river with silver burning
in its veins, the earth rich and needful as it is,
a true *swaraj* of absolute instances.

swaraj: self-rule

149

Slack

After the long etceteras of the flooding tide,
before the surf rattles back through the beach's knucklebones,
the sea's fallow is as still as the twist of milk
which Vermeer's milkmaid tips slowly and for ever
from a jug to a shallow bowl.

The fishing-boats winched to the top of the shore for winter
lie awkwardly stern on to the steely horizon,
stranded in the damp acoustic of an amnesty
declared between past and future, where all storms
approach as smothered thunder.

Calm of a kind – but unnerving, like the serene
gaze of Piero's pregnant madonna, whose hand
resting on her belly must already feel, above
the unbroken waters, the stirrings of a mortal god,
the hard place of the skull.

Threshold

Here nothing is certain, there will be no hour
of arrival, no imperative of departure.

All too often the sun wastes its power
in a blank oblong which slants across the floor.

She looks back from the open door to the bed,
but is she thinking *still*, *not yet* or *already?*

Those petite ankles, the red shoes with their straps –
you feel for her, whatever may not happen.

She waits, in her shiny hat. A train trawls
the misty horizon. The door stands there, yawning.

150

Familiars
(for Erica)

The relic

In a desk drawer
among loose shuffles
of receipts, old diaries,
chequebook stubs,
photos, strange keys,
it surfaces now
and then – a long
blonde scimitar
of shorn hair
warm to the touch,
not plaited
for a locket or ring
but disgracefully casual,
just lightly bound
with a blue ribbon:
and is somehow shocking,
like finding the sun
adrift for ever
in an endless sky.

A daughter's dream

As the black gale crashed
into the flinching fir-trees
on the hill behind the house
she told me the secret
of her first bad dream:
the eyeball, her own, being sliced
open – she could see it happening –
by a bright searing scalpel.

Enter the triangular facets
of a cut brilliant: her inheritance
of split vision recurring,
of a name under a name.

Sister and brother

When she was small, it was easy for him
to put his higher arm round her
as the early pictures show: and even
the one where he seems to be choking her
in her pram has always been understood
as a show of brotherly affection.

At Pendeen, near the two black foghorns
rearing seaward, they are standing together
in a field, holding hands. That must have been
the last undivided summer. Later,
it is always her with an arm round him.

Subtractions

The family mathematics are simple:
now and again take one away.
One from a set of spoons, leaving five,
One from a family of four: three stay.

The one subtracted has a different name
at different times: great-granny absconding
with milk fever, or a father met
rarely, or a mother there and gone.

One alone in a house with two women,
one alone in a house with two men,
one alone in a hospital bed,
one alone, starting again.

Carried over

That Christmas, she even let me
give her a piggyback, since she was shoeless,
to show her the black atomic berries
of the ivy, its frosted umbels high
up on the wall – and close to them
the sugary white and pink rims
of a single iceberg rose. Thus
she carries me over time's thresholds.

As If

As if borne up on some angelic thermal
to a point from which the body of the earth
explained itself entirely in sunlit distance –
the fields patched with crops, swelling and falling
within their mesh of hedgerows; a peaceable column
of smoke from somewhere stretching upwards, thinning;
the towers and the rubble of cities brought together
as a working map; the fringes of the sea laid
out in white at the foot of the far horizon.

As if you were not still waiting here, at the edge
of a shorn field of fire, for the barrier to lift
and, with luck, for the surly guard to wave you on
past the spindly watchtowers and the freshly turned earth
into another country where you may not settle.

Sloes

No lack of present wonders –
the rowan's star-showers
stopped with blood,
the polished ochre
of acorns, some
clamped in their cups,
or the pungent sapwood
locked into each tight bead of holly.

But the darkest amazements of all
in the bright scour
of autumn riches
are the sloes that hang
among wicked spines,
their blue-black skin
misted with a bloom
like breath staying on a flawless mirror.

Cutting one open, you find
a simple pulp
of greeny yellow,
weak moonlight,
and a single nubble
bedded in blister-water,
a bone-hard core,
an oubliette that beggars belief.

From somewhere, the purest birdsong –
last flarings
of the cherished light.
Always you return
to the sloe, to test
the coinage, to conjure
from its sour heart
the future perfect of its white flowers.

Estuarial
(for Kevin and Linda)

Cormorant and heron preside
over shiny flanks of sleech.
Sky becomes more and more
of an issue. Light promotes
itself in oystery silver,
pink and grey.

Out in the open at last,
away from that green darkness
of upstream, that waltzing drift
of madness, where bluebells blurred
everything and the salmon leapt
rigid into air.

And not yet swept out past
the land's faltering goodbyes
of chevroned huts, a frayed
red flag, to the first
tufts of spray, the great hoop
of the homeless horizon.

Boats nod at their moorings.
Trains come and go
blindly, huge and leaning
on their curves. Low walls
hold back the onlooking shores
where silence is a settlement.

Here, too, there are still
secret transactions – between
the last of fresh water
and the inroading tides; or
summer heat and the constant
burning of the heart.

An Organ Recital

Even before we reached the Impromptu by Vierne,
in fact during the Prelude and Fugue in E Flat
by Bach (J.S.) – the key, it is thought, representing
the Trinity, as might also the three main subjects
of both prelude and fugue – my heart started
its tricks, its random *fugato* of racing flurries.

I thought of the echocardiogram, its absurd
pictures – of, for instance, the mitral valve with its flap
of something that could have been skin or stretched gum
and which lifted, wavered about and somehow flopped
back into place. I already had my own picture
of the atrium, all that blood pouring in from the veins.

Meanwhile, however, in the windchest the stickers opened
and closed the pallets on orders transmitted by
the backfalls and trackers. Draw-stops moved the sliders.
The swell-box waggled its Venetian shutters, the couplers
linked pedals with great. While the flue pipes thundered,
the reeds continued to flutter their metal tongues.

Such hidden systems, such faith in synchronism!
And all this even before we reached the Impromptu
by Vierne. Impromptu – literally, on the spur
of the moment. Louis Vierne, the French composer
and organist who, blind from birth, died
in the middle of playing the organ in Notre Dame.

For Jon Silkin

The flowers of your poems persist –
and each must answer to its name,
its own nature: dandelion,
a bluebell, lilies of the valley,
peonies, the strawberry plant,
a daisy, crowfoot in water,
the violet, milkmaids, moss,
goat's-beard and daisy, harebell.

They will not be bound as a garland
or pinched to a wreath: it is
their natural wealth which carries
your voice. Under your lodestar
with its pointed demands – to be exact,
yet various; to judge, yet to love;
to wander, yet believe in home –
they bud and blossom endlessly.

Kaddish

This is a song of a song gone missing
in which children were fearless and ran
straight for the eye of the wobbly camera,
put out their tongues and waved their hands.

This is also the raw edge of music
the black intervals' virtual dissonance
in which the violin almost remembers
how once it played for weddings and dances.

In the missing song, grown-ups were kind
and parents there to run into, always –
mother in the dress that smelt of safety,
father taking pictures of family holidays.

Here is the way back never to be taken
to the peaceable kingdom of praise and thanks
where all puffs of gunsmoke simply exploded
into lightsome feathers, and all bullets were blanks.

This is a song of a song gone missing,
with words simple as pebbles, inferring
a sense that the mind can no longer admit
or the heart still quite unlearn.

Allotments in Winter

The plots shrink in their drenched sorrows to a scrawl
of husks and hanks, the blackened heads of sunflowers,
with a small flourish of ice-plant here or there,
some bushes dotted with a few berries:
like the sketchy outlines of a story which could in time
acquire the status of a minor classic, whose ending
might be uncertain, but would still give some credence
to delight and the word fleshed in detail –
the ribbing of the wheelbarrow's tyre printed onto mud,
the clang of the spade striking a spark from stone,
the poplars' last highlights that wave all day
from a sky scoured to brightness for tomorrow.

3

Out of Silence

It is the silence of the world that is real
THOMAS MERTON

Beneath the civic gardens and the roots
of plants, under the blue fumes,
the darkness at first reports nothing
to displace the world above,
or its cold air nipped by the cries of finches.

But change follows change: the threshold turns
to a corridor, then to a room filled
with a morse of footsteps tapping overhead,
then comes the rush of a drowning downpour,
resolved as a pool where every ripple
converges to drain away at the centre,
leaving only the red earth. The water
brought to nothing, and with it
the flesh and all its working parts.

Yet here, in the starless sump of the city,
the siren songs of its weathered people
are held on stems of silence that prove
unbreakable: black frequencies
that fill and empty, fill again.

*

*Nibbana – the cooling of the fire, the calming of the wind, the settled
quality and sensitivity of still water*
VENERABLE SUCITTO BHIKKU

The wind gets up slyly – flicks a bud,
tests a twig, the dip of a branch,
dies away to nothing and begins again.

In its middle period it edges down
chimneys, puffing dark soot into rooms,
twangs wires, volleys some birds over hedges,
dies away to nothing and begins again.

Until it roars in the high fir trees,
rams the isobars together, knocks
ships into rattling cupboards, the waves
into furious slopes of marble whipped with spindrift.

Until it slackens for a few moments,
releases its grip on the hunched cyclist,
removes its support from the figure leaning
into it, then buffets them both back to the strain.

Until, sooner or later, it collapses
and the blossom no longer trembles, its petals
as if already fallen to the cloud-bright water.

*

Don't forget Valentine's Day
NOTICE SUSPENDED IN SUPERMARKET

Goodbye hope to see you again soon
All night the unspoken words
track across the screens
of the checkouts – all retail romances
demand that goodbye is hello,
that shopping is what goes on
happily ever after
hope to see you

All is well, beneath
the unblinking harvest lights –
the meats are covered with paper,
the shelves restocked, thousands
of gleaming bottles rub shoulders,
plenty walks down the aisles
see you again

Here all noise has been channelled
into ducts, or the phlegmy dozing
of constant refrigeration,
here is the world in a chain
of brands, of air-freighted seasons,
each place a clone of everywhere
again soon

You must not think that gorse
is out of bloom, that anyone
is sobbing in a corner, afraid
that kissing is out of season,
or that something has been forgotten
though endlessly repeated
soon goodbye hope
Goodbye hope to see you again soon

*

Oh silence, independent of a stopped ear,
You observe birds, flying, sing with wings instead
DAVID WRIGHT

All these stories are waiting
in the mind, on the tip of the tongue,
to be told with the precious lips
and the true language of the hands:

how the leaves failed in their rustling
and the birdsong died away
taking conversation with it;

how later, cars stopped even
purring, and pneumatic drills
were pure vibration that crazed
the tarmac and quaked the flesh;

how planes would come unstuck
without a sound, lifting
to beg the simple air;

how, last of all, a rocket
rose from a cushion of flame,
its wake a billow of brightness
and the sky, a great blue ear
into which the silence spiralled.

*

*The name of Oradour indicates that from the Roman period there was
there an altar and a place to offer prayers for the dead... Alas, it could
never have better deserved the name it received*
GUIDE TO ORADOUR

No silence less elected than these –
the silence of the tailor's sewing-machine
the silence of the garage workshop
the silence of the rasping trams
the silence of the hotel cutlery
the silence of the burnt church
the silence of the cleaver
on the butcher's board
the silence of the school
Oradour

The silence of the ladle
in the silver tureen
the silence of watches stopped
at the last time of day
the silence of passbooks
the silence of family photos
the silence shut into barns
the silence of witnessing silence
the silence we carry in our blood
Oradour

*

There, where the long street roars, hath been
The stillness of the central sea
TENNYSON

Duck-egg or cobalt, pillars of cloud,
mackerel, mare's tails, a field of open blue –
away from the flare of mustard pitched on the cliff,
the sky takes out its options on the view.

The sea has its own work to do, lifting
the swell, and handing boats from here to there –
or magnifying raindrops to pools that bubble
as if all the fish in the world were sippling the air.

And once in a blue moon, the horizon
vanishes, leaving the boats to struggle, snared
like black insects in a dove-grey mesh: and the sun
a pearl set in silence, the sea and the sky's blank stare.

*

Even if you don't win you can't lose
BINGO HALL PROMOTIONAL OFFER

This is the shape which outdoes word or number,
the shadow free of desire and regret,
but not the round face of alarm or wonder,
not the sun rising or the moon setting,
not the alpha, not the omega,
not a halo or a spangled dome,
but the O of your dreams, a thought balloon
circular as a reel of film projecting
the life to be lived for ever, and soon,
round as a cannonball breaching the ring
of everyday worries, round as a bubble
that rises, shining, clear of trouble:
the O in fortune you watch as it tracks
your progress. From the basket your own face stares back.

*

Great Streets of Silence led away
To Neighborhoods of Pause
EMILY DICKINSON

Outside, the noise of traffic like a clean sweep:
here, the tick of wood, the cobwebbed window,
the dew-lipped flowers, the bulrush of the bellrope.
Air slack in the organ-pipes: Gabriel leaning
across to Mary, across the golden arrowheads
of morning light. Something is always waiting
to be disclosed, to be received, that cannot
be rushed or delayed, that has to find its moment.

Till then, the candles still not budding into flame,
the authority of the atmosphere barely challenged,
the joyous dove still kept from hurtling earthward,
the slightest of breezes wafting the hanging fringes
of the altar-cloth. All day, the traffic outside.
The traverse of sunlight. The least echo worked on
by silence, by the faithful worm of silence.

*

I will make you brooches and toys for your delight
of bird-song at morning and star-shine at night
ROBERT LOUIS STEVENSON

Moonfire catching each crystal in the rock,
silence attracting attention to itself,
stones measuring the knowledge they lack –
when the blurry fleece of mist lifted off,
every feature was made an example:
the stars, the corroding frost, even
the amber-eyed flock of milling sheep
which passed through deepest moon-shadow as if
dumbstruck, without any hope of bleating.

Further east, between the shoulders
of the hills I, too, was dazzled by darkness,
eyes bruised by staring, with only
the fraught river to take at its word.
And what were words to make of the stars,

166

so many and flagrant, green, white, red,
that burst through so suddenly, cloud-clearing?

Only later, when the dawn dipped down
into the valley, came the sense of a song –
one intimated but not yet begun,
the blank pages of a notebook lying
open, rinsed in a fervour of light.
Slowly the landscape started to advance,
at first still wearing the green and black
of night-time. And then the birds began,
their high songs plentiful as the stars.

*

You cannot solder an Abyss
With Air
EMILY DICKINSON

As if in a dream, the chestnut trees
fall away, their turrets shrinking.
Below, threading the early mist,
birds reduced to tiny floaters
bathe in the great ocean of the air.

You would not need to be a god
to love a planet captured like this –
the sweet logic of the fields etched
with the plough's cursor, racetracks, cities,
each in its place; a hum of traffic
on miles of good roads; a dog barking;
and every fault a feature of sense.

What holds is a balance struck between
the roar of the frayed uplifting flame
and the drift of silence, that pear-drop shadow
which swells and darkens with each inch of fall
back to the solid, hollow ground beneath.

The Enclosures

Four unexpected meadow flowers slide out from
the sky-blue letter you sent from Kyrgyzstan –
a clover with pink bristles, a blue vetch
faded to light mauve, a yellow crucifer,
a white chickweed. They lie here, tiny, flattened,
intact – as delicate as any of the wreaths
found buried with the ithyphallic boy-king
and all his rubble of riches: the collarette
with little love-apples and berries of woody nightshade
strung on strips of palm; or the farewell garland
of olive leaves, blue water-lily petals
and cornflowers, which someone left on the dark threshold.
    These, too, paling with absence, recast love's spell
    as open pathos, and time as immortelles.

FROM **EYE-BABY**

(2006)

Bosnia, 1996

This is the fridge. It lives in the garden
with its door open, alongside the gaping
jaw of the car plundered for parts.
Both are close to the burnt vines.

This, you can tell, is a private house.
You know by the scorch marks above the window frames,
the blackened roof-beams, the way that explosions
have skewed the whole thing on its broken foundations.

This is the bridge. On either side
it dips into the river as if,
trying to open the wrong way up,
it had fallen into its own reflection.

This is the night, where a black dog
lies curled awake, lacking the heart
to bark or sleep. There is unpicked fruit
on a tree whose name not many know.

These are American believers, going
To Medugorje. They are full of joy.
Each one is wearing a badge printed
with the words *Mary's Faithful Pilgrim.*

These marks on the ground are known today
As Sarajevo roses. They are what is left
when mortars are fired into a queue
of people waiting to buy bread.

These loud shouts are coming from people
driven to madness by the war, by grief.
Unlike those who have stepped on land-mines,
they still have legs and run through the streets.

The Glimmering

The horizon draws the line
at having been tamped down
all through a slutchy autumn,
moves in as a caul
of rain which blears the hills,
hissing like the prefix that history
adds to words and laughter:
finally, shrinks to the glimmering
from under a stable door,
a straw-breadth of light which can only
imply the warmth of spring
or the memory of it – the long
pursed buds of the lily
peeling open on the angel's wand.

Scale

The pod of a boat
seed or kernel
braves the dark water,
riding the limitless flux,
insisting on the small-scale –
water scooped up
in a cupped hand:
a measure.

Notes for the Ship's Log

(for Peter Scupham)

1

Such is the course steered across
the cunning theatre of the sea, with its deft
transformations, from first word to last,
indefinite to imperative.

2

Cargo of common dust, quintessence
of all that rises and falls: the manifest
drawn up to allow for any number
of possible shapes and guises.

3

Un peu d'histoire for sure, the memory's
box-room of toys: and assorted structures
from hutments to outrageous palaces
of purest sugar-candy.

4

Passage made through the nightmare tropics,
the lush green fields of calenture
laid wavily out as far as the horizon,
tempting to lie down in.

5

Hallucinations brought on, perhaps,
by rancid lobscouse: and, persisting,
the realisation that we are headed
beyond the projected world.

6

As ultimate promotion of dust, the presence
of ghosts gathered, at dusk, in the rooms
of the dying. Their endless patience. The weight
of their commanding absences.

7

Many, by now, the figures on deck,
their faces upturned, as if questing:
as if they knew that Ararat must be
a landfall of saving words.

Stowaways

Blind passengers, reduced
to pure anxiety, their spirits
rise and fall with each lift
and plunge of the butting hull:
bracing themselves, they test
the strength of their old visions.

Some, discovered after food
has gone missing from the galley,
or given away by a whiff
of tobacco seeping through a bulkhead,
are simply tipped overboard
as if they were so much trash.

Others, airborne, are undone
by cold – cold which unpicks,
finger by numbed finger,
their hold on a strut, slides them,
helpless, out from the wheelbay
into a shroud of thin air.

Falling through cloud or water,
perhaps their last recall
is the iron taste of blood,
the danger of not leaving,
or the far horizon bright
and burnished as New Jerusalem.

What is certain becomes so
only late on, when the stowaways
re-emerge, insistent phantoms,
at the point where memory rounds
on experience, and well within sight
of the dark relief of land.

Altdorfer's *Saint George and the Dragon*

The dying beast
has become absurd,
a deflated puffball,
its energy collapsed to
a cartoon of dismay

It has nothing to compare
with the swelling rump
of the white charger,
its impatient hooves
and proud head

Or the darkly glinting
armour of the knight
slumped in the saddle,
exhausted or at ease,
his lance lowered

The knight, around whom
the Hercynian forest
deploys its huge splays,
its world-wall which will reach
from earth to sky

A Response to Rothko

A picture lives by companionship,
expanding and quickening in the eyes
of the sensitive observer. It dies
by the same token.

Transgressions of the frame: the subject leaning
its elbow out of the canvas. The cloak's
crimson lining that spills,
molten, onto wood.

And *vice versa*, the nightmare world
sucked in, banged up in a box, glazed:
here, the worst of horror
is drained of blood.

By the same token, the citizens of art's
republic of loneliness struggle towards
hope, a horizon beyond
the surrounding truths.

King and Queen
(for Ivan and Lissa Campbell)

This is the story: as the sculptor played with a bit
of modelling wax, it became a head with horns
and a beard. As soon as the horns turned to a crown
he recognised the head of a king, who would need
a queen, to be complete.

For fifty years they have sat on their bench of stone,
looking out from the shelter of each other. Knowledge
is a slight curvature of the spine; patience, the sky
and its lights caught in the single eye each has,
passing endlessly on.

South is their kingdom, where moonlight cannot reach
the blurred suburbs of sunken cities; where clouds
languish over African forests, and wolves are so rare
they must be a wavy mirage born of the intense
white-out of noonday heat.

South where you two, as your photos show, masquerade
as regal alter egos, figures languidly reclining
on Moroccan sand: one stylishly stretched out,
the other sitting at ease, calm and smiling
into the uncertain haze.

As if you already sensed that an expedition
begun with love, with luck would find the way
which leads from double vision to a singular view,
from desert to desire, mirage to marriage – a story
less of discovery than recognition.

In the Auction House

Somewhere between the idea
and the dry tap of the hammer,
in the long traverse from author
to auction, from pen to paddle,
time and chance have rendered
whole lives to lots.

In this there is less of Larkin
with his England *going, going,*
soon gone – and more, perhaps,
of Thor's hammer as it swings
in Heaney's *North*, between
geography and trade.

Enter, too, the auctioneer
from *Moortown*, described by Hughes –
a man with cattle to sell
to reluctant bidders who know
history and the distance between
worth and price.

But even those Devon farmers
might be frankly amazed
at what can be penned, as here,
together under one roof –
on this floor, for instance, a currency
entirely of paper:

while upstairs, seated at the virginals,
is a young woman whose price
must surely outfly all guesswork –
her yellow shawl ballooning
as if suddenly caught up
by a feverish squall.

Surrealist Negatives

No engine advances on air from the boarded fireplace,
the flames are out on the fine neck of the giraffe,
the seven drawers ascending the woman are shut.
On the stairs, all the figures but one have completed
their descent successfully. No telephone is caught
in the lobster pots. No black flags are billowing
on the shore of the dream. No unblinking eye
wags from side to side on the metronome.
Donkeys are safe, the forests and cities re-peopled.
The urinal is once again connected to the plumbing.
The glass of water is just what it says it is.
Everything has been invented, nothing discovered.

La Mouche de Holub

Dans le langage corporel de leur propre profession
les objets peuvent garder leur unique image
de pot, arbre, marée empiétant –
et même les ailes de la mouche de Holub,
au lustre vert-de-noir, peuvent rester intactes
en passant par *fly, Fliege, sinek, mosca,*
tous les Babel des désignations humaines.

Mais faire que le son et le rythme précis
du vol franchissent sans dommage les frontières
de l'air, accompagnés des silences qu'invoque
chaque mot placé par la langue – parvenir
à convertir en présent le passé que recèle
toute traduction: c'est ça qui assure
que le cerveau du traducteur ne cesse jamais de vrombir.

Holub's Fly

In the body language of their stated selves
objects may keep their singular image
as pot, tree, the inroading tide –
and even the wings of Holub's fly,
with their green-black gloss, be held intact
through *mouche, Fliege, sinek, mosca,*
all the Babels of human naming.

But to have the exact sound and rhythm
of its flight borne safely over the frontiers
of air, along with the silences invoked
by each word tongued – somehow, to make
of the past concealed in all translation
a present tense: it's that which keeps
the translator's mind endlessly buzzing.

Sparrowgrass
(for Helen)

Butter-wet, lickerous,
tender tongue-tie,
wilt-headed fasces,
maytime mouth-melt,
work of the fingers,
lips and tongue,
more a bird
in hand than in the bush –
and offering a way
to recover a baby's
unashamed delight,
afterwards, by sucking
each finger clean.

White Peach

Under the skin,
itself rose soft
but tough, bitter,
the flesh, firm
yet tender
to the knife,
dense with sugars

The flesh, white
not yellow,
white at the border
of green, the colour
of iceberg roses,
with the pallor of illness
at its most alluring

Long before
you reach the stone-heart
with its hard ridges,
you will be up
to your elbows
in runnels of juice,
your fingers dripping

And memory, turned
informer, will tell
that you know already
this bitter-sweetness
you fear and desire –
the linger of it
on your drenched lips

From Petra

1

Whole cliff-faces worn
wondrously by the hot wind
to mottled rashers of stone

Yet across the thresholds
nothing but silence, less
soft than the rock, echoless

Space meagrely scooped,
a baffle of darkness, culs-de-sac,
not even the way to Avernus

A darkness from which to turn
back to the shrinking shadows
of noonday, the beating light

Even, to suffer in silence
the long persistence of the flies
raging all round your head

2

There is something between
the rockface and the eye
some interference
a veil of white threads
or finely scratched glass

What is observed
is far from solid,
far from impossible,
a city engulfed,
cire perdue

Or a seal worn down
unevenly, pressed
into the wax
of the molten rock
and, slightly, blurring

Still readable
are porticoes, pediments,
involuted
crenellations,
emerging or fading

It glows less
rose-red than pink,
the colour you might
imagine for the inside
walls of a dream

Fountains

Part of the culture,
you could say, with a backdrop
of lavish palaces,
triumphalist boulevards,
extravagant gardens.
And apt for disguises –
shaving-brush bristles
of foam, plumes,
sly squirts
from the mouths of dolphins
or the necks of urns,
or arcing back
in a little boy's
stream of piss.

Water that splatters
back to the surface,
plentiful, ready
to resume itself,
to be used as a template
for shape, again
and again, like words –
the way that a poem
by Apollinaire
might flower on the page
as a spray or fountain.

But already the basin
is drying out,
the pipework starting
to choke. Soon
there will be little
but the crackle of leaves
brittle as pappadums,
scraping on stone.

Sensed

1

At the turn of the path
where the earth becomes dusty...

Where is the thinking ghost,
the shadow self?

Each chime of the clock
a dent hammered into
the smooth surface of dreaming

And the thick fragrance
of night-flowers flooding the garden...

Who is lying, heart racing,
in the room with drawn curtains?

At the turn of the path
where the trees close in
all your possible dreams are hidden

2

The wind falters in the leaves
a voice trailing
into forgetfulness

Hanks of rain drive
over the dark
lure of the lake

Hardly to be glimpsed, a hand
draws heavy
curtains closer

In the leaves, the wind begins
to stir again, squaring
up to the night

In a Dream
(for Elizabeth)

Two people on a West Yorkshire hillside,
sitting side by side on a wall, dangling
their legs over the edge, like kids.
Someone says, very softly, *I love you.*
Someone else leans a head on a shoulder.
They look straight ahead, at the chestnut trees
Hanging their splays over dusty ground.

And someone knows that, just out of sight
below the wall, even this far inland,
seethes an ocean of storms which will never
subside: and is at a loss how to tell
the innocent other, or even how
to wake to the possible consequence
of putting such happiness at risk.

Catechism

What are you looking at?
The baffle in your eye.

What do you see?
The depths of the real.

How are you justified?
Hardly, if at all.

Where are your parents?
Buried apart.

Where is your wife?
In forgotten dreams.

Where are your children?
Escaped to their lives.

Of whom do you dream now?
Too many to name.

What do you give?
Too little, too much.

What do you take?
Too much, not enough.

How long have you got?
Too little for redress.

What things make you glad?
Too many to count.

What makes you ashamed?
Inaction, excuses.

What makes you lament?
The world's madnesses.

What makes you hopeful?
Those who try.

Anything else?
The love in your eye.

In the Bar Italia
(for Erica)

You could say, with reason, that almost
nothing is happening beyond
the flicking of the overhead fan,
its languorous division of the air
into blades of shadow and light.

The beige formica refuses
either to absorb or reflect,
the slowly revolving spiral
of coffee lies perfectly wound
into the bubbled froth.

In her momentary absence
it comes upon him, a force
of feeling enough, almost,
to jump him sideways for joy.

Alalia

The moment before the dodgem car
slews to a halt,
when pumping the pedal
does nothing: all power gone.

Some of the dying do not
speak when they reach
this point of truth;
as if they had seen through something.

Neither do they invite
queries. The people
who are in the room
will simply go on waiting.

As the room alters around them:
as the ghosts also
wait. As the room
softly becomes an anteroom.

And here, swinging from car
to car, comes the man
with the wide grin
to collect everybody's money.

At the Bedside

Perhaps it is not, after all,
the whole story which races
through the heads of the dying, with the gloss
of last words in waiting –
but some inconsequential detail
which just happens to have stuck.

Say, for instance, the taste
of a boiled egg eaten, when a child,
in St Austell, by a window looking
out over kaolin mountains.
The sweetness of the yolk against
the tangy bread and butter.

Or the perfect round of apples
at the foot of a tree in Brittany
so scrawny as to make fruit seem
miraculous. It looked as if
it had shed them all at once
as a single golden earth-halo.

Or the view of the old bridge
at Mostar, its high brow
soaring and swooping above
the Neretva. Or the drugging smell
of red valerian, or the feel
of silk rubbed between the fingers.

But perhaps such images are only
the journeys of wishing and warding
for those who wait by the bed,
for whom also it is late,
and who cannot ignore the tut
and sigh of the morphine shunt.

The Edge: Remembering Romano

This year more than ever, it seems,
the house is festooned with swooping birdsong;
longer than ever the vines' twisting travels,
heavier their fruit in the weighing hand;
deeper the evening glow on the stubble,
keener the bladed light on the earth;
taller the spill of the olive tree, broader
the jigsaw of fig-leaves close to the pool.

And part of all this is the force of your smile,
your love of giving, the brimming armfuls
of melons or lettuce, your lively alliance
with everything natural, everything quick:
greater than ever the real value
of your gone presence giving fullness its edge.

A Holiday Snap

Thirty summers ago, on a dusty footpath
somewhere in the Dolomites, the air
heavy with heat and resin, he must have turned
round and thought what a good picture it would make –

his mother in her red cardigan, white blouse
and blue denim skirt, making her way gingerly
down a rough stairway of slate, dwarfed between
the surrounding forest's soaring pillars of fir trees.

Somehow the camera saw more than he bargained for –
when the prints came back, no gloss could disguise
how small she was, how vulnerable despite
the pluck and cheerfulness she'd always shown.

It was all here – the irritable duets,
his intolerance, her fine traps of tears,
the choking closeness of home, the old progression
of anger, guilt, anger at guilt: but now

for the first time, and long before her death,
he saw, in one sharp frame, how little he could help her
as she made her way through angled shade and sunlight,
the loose slate skittering on itself under her feet.

From *And yet* to *As if*

And yet... at this precise moment
the brake goes on, the scale swings back
to even Stevens, at both ends
of the seesaw feet squirm in the air,
the *via media* staking its claim:
the fulcrum hefts a double weight,
the trimmer balances the rocking
boat, poets balance their books.

And precisely after this moment comes
the adrenaline rush, the craving for an outright
refusal, the urge to kick over tables,
lob glasses at the cowardly barman,
stomp outside to shout home truths
at the blue moon, before escaping
in a drunken boat headed for the last
isle of sweet excesses... *As if.*

Reprise

Your friends have taken to telling you
tales about yourself – for instance,
how once you led the way
at night into a closed
and dusty alpine hotel,
where you slept in the ghostly ballroom
and fell through the rotted joists.

Or how, one summer Sunday,
you were caught in the rain together
in a small skiff, and took shelter
under the arch of a bridge
where you ate a bagful of sweets
and anything might have happened.

And someone else has never
forgotten the words exchanged
apparently when you met him
coming out of the cinema
in Walton Street, on the day
that Kennedy was shot.

And even the voice of a stranger
reminds you that when he left
you told him to keep in touch,
which is why he is ringing now
in the hope of coming to see you
with the family – just a few nights.

This is simply what the past
can still do, the way it takes you
on to reprise or reprisal,
or re-invents you deftly
in the errors memory makes:
adjusting its facets, collecting
enough anecdotes for a wake.

Twin Babies Waking

Rose

Drumming the air
with all four limbs
rigid, goes with
the daily manifesto's
exultant shout.

Such force, given
the proper attachments,
could surely power
a moderate village, or
a one-woman orchestra.

Grace

The world is there
to be observed,
taken in, studied,
its textures tested
one by one.

The day begins
with a slight frown
indicating that work
on the great research project
has now resumed.

Feeding the Dolls

The two year olds
are feeding their dolls
air sandwiches
crammed with promises –
and brought at a run
from the bright kitchen
endlessly stocked
with imagination
and their delight.

The dolls are sitting
in bloated collapse,
stomachs out,
heads hanging –
as over-full
as the hog flung
down from the ramparts
of Carcassonne
to show the besiegers
that there really was
food to spare
in the suffering city.

Working Back

The future has arrived, a preview
in the form of two girl putti –
two, since you'd no more expect it
to be single, than think that a cyclops
would be much good at squinting.

They entertain each other
with possibilities, invent
new noises, improbable
hand gestures, take it in turns
to act the part of echo.

Lying back in the bath
after a hairwash, they look
as driftily composed as Ophelia,
their features ruffed in foam.
They do not understand death.

But still they like to align
alternatives, rehearse
the little mantra which explains:
Mummy out, Daddy here
or *Mummy here, Daddy gone.*

If one wakes in tears,
the other looking anxiously on,
it is not a matter of pain
but the shock of losing a dream.
They are working back to the present.

The Puzzle

And the word made bone was at first
the budding frame of a baby
in its baggy skin:
and dwelt among us, easily
outlasting its quilt of flesh.

In time it also became
evidence beyond contention –
fractured, stove in
or set out on shelves, an index
of bundled tibias and skulls.

Wobble-headed child
of Christmas, supine or propped
on blue, trying
to frown the world into focus,
for you this is yet to come:

the puzzle of how to read
the non-identical twins
of judgement and love,
how to count the broken bones
and still reach out for rejoicing.

Syringa

Cutesy, with that ra-ra frill
at the hem of each flower –
and you've clearly been using
eye make-up again, to give
that bruised and needy look.
And some, no doubt, would think well
of those anthers prinked with yellow.

It can't last, of course,
a few downpours
will be enough
to burn your soft skin brown.
But by then, forget flirtation –
one whiff of you, and the garden
is crammed with lost souls.

Blue Iris

You flower in tatters,
your yellow and blue
rainbow polarities
an ensign run up
from bladed leaves
after a struggle.

There is something unflower-like
about you, and dangerously
exposed, as the twist
of your tubers is exposed,
even something
unbecoming.

Your flame continues
to flicker from
its last redoubt
of washed blue.
That, also, is
imprinted on the eye.

A Travellers' Tale

After the dusty nightmare drive through the mountains
where roadside shrines leaned with their little doors
sagging open, and rusted cars were breaking
out of time on the plunging scree, they came
to Apollonia, where the dusklight had already retired
to its misty retreat on the lake.

Not speaking Greek, they wandered like vacant dreamers
past the warm coronas of candles glimpsed through the portal
of a church, then on through a few lit stalls displaying
honey, halva and fruit, drawn by a waft
of music to a ring of trees with whitewashed trunks
where some dancers were calmly swaying.

All of them wore black – and not one, you'd guess,
was under seventy: absorbed, knowing each step,
they moved with ease yet seemed a world away,
enclosed in their own rhythms… The travellers found
a place to eat, and ordered what they wanted
by pointing, since they could not say.

On the way back to their cheap hotel, they discovered
the dancers gone, and silence guarding their absence
with a version of power the still air could not define.
A few yards on, the church stood in darkness, folded
shut. That night they hardly slept, and rose early
to escape the mosquitoes' whining.

It was only when they got close to the border, with nothing
to declare, that they sensed just how far they had gone
out of their way, on a loop past age and youth
through a zone of forgiving ghosts where acceptance seemed
common as goosegrass, and love itself an eye-baby
dancing in the eye of truth.

As a Bird

Whether or not you agree that it's fair to describe
the imagination as a bird, here it goes again
in its flight of fancy mode, lifting up and away
from the city streets – the food outlets, the stink
of pot pourri in gift shops, *Big Issue* sellers,
sharp-suited men briefed to market the truth,
bargain hunters, and the homeless, lying on the green.

The fine cathedral itself is swiftly reduced
to a stand-up model which must surely be held together
with tucked-in flanges and glue. The imagination
soon has the whole of Devon in its view –
the working sump of the moor, the delving combes,
the light-fissured rivers, the two coasts cushioned in foam,
the seamarks, the loom of lights beneath the horizon.

Even time, at this remove, is no more
a problem than space – in Teignmouth, for example,
sunk in a Mexican wave of wind-driven rain,
John Keats is still nursing poor Tom, while further north
Ted Hughes continues to take the elemental
brunt of underworlds, and track the spirits
which quicken Shakespeare, salmon, fox and flower.

And just across the border, three silhouettes
outlined against the great dish of the moon
in its summer fullness, are high on the rich air
of the Quantocks. Imagination chooses to place
Coleridge in the lead, garrulous, ecstatic –
with brother and sister Wordsworth doing their best
to keep up, while avoiding roots and rabbit-holes.

Sooner or later, though, there has to be
a coming down to earth, a confrontation
with the blank veto of paper or screen, the tug
of need and background noise. What you then must imagine
is coaxing that bird down from the air, still singing:
and a way somehow to take your true bearings,
to find in the word, even this late on, a beginning.

At the Turn

Nothing is set
at nought, or seems
to come of age:
in the garden, a pert
blackbird chips
at silence, a whiff
of camphor comes off
the smoke tree glowing
in its long late blush.

Its leaves flare
from green to acid
yellow, with veins
which stay red
and so fine
they could not be immune
to hurt. Then they turn
crimson, magenta,
blood-red, murrey.

Now, as they break
away, it is clear
how utter, uncountable
they are: how time
alone could not measure
each one
turning in its glory
as it drifts down
to the dark earth.

NEW POEMS
(2010)

Edenic

(Kettle's Yard, Cambridge)

Yet there are such places
of the outside-in
dream of order,
where every gift
of the light is more
than its parts and each
part remains whole in itself.

And here is one, conjured
by a tug on the bell-rope
– the locus of pigments
in bloom, stone's
coiled energy,
the irreducible
grain that runs through
worked and unworked wood.

In the mind's traverse which links
the maker's hand
and the viewer's eye,
or the distant shore
and this inland calm,
what is it that gives
each instance its weight,
the full glow of nature?

Just so, this little vase
of lilies of the valley
on a round table;
this cup worn
by usage; even
the book left splayed
at this or this page
by a reader who might return.

It is nothing less than retrieval,
the gift of attention
that slows the pulse
to proper health –
the material world
held to account
by the soul, and not found wanting.

Chickweed

Simple as any wish –
to take on into winter
such modesty, recalled
from the already dark
verges of summer:
those stars, sparse
and profuse, unparticular
yet keeping measure,
scintillae of the spirit,
white sparks that fly
upward to join
the very idea of spring.

The Place Itself

Here is another story gone missing,
in which the road taken and the road not taken
both lead to the same destination:
where what was once half tumbled has become
deliberate incompleteness, and the forest
advances on what is left of narration.

Whatever can be named – wild boar, mosquitoes,
seedling ash trees slowly on the make,
can have no part in anything more
than pure contingency: and the mill itself,
marooned on its mamelon, declines to be
either a ruin or a poet's tower.

Looking in at the door, you look
through and out: climbing the stairs,
you'd swear they thrust out from the wall one by one
as you need them. Up past the storm lanterns hanked
like onions, you find that the roof is a silo,
a coolie's hat warding off sky and sun.

Neither onymous, nor heading back
to airy nothing, entirely faithful
to itself, the place impels lightness, giddy
laughter, the opening of bottles. The children
dance round it, knowing, pretend to collide
and end up in the numinous grove of a god.

Portuguese Sonnet

I am a secret orchestra whose instruments strum and bang inside me.
I only know myself in the symphony.
FERNANDO PESSOA

Firstly, just doodles of language, loose noise to test
each possible echo, and not yet deadened by
real frontiers: the merest outputs of breath,
not to be taken seriously. But already
across the growing thresholds of mind and mouth
nursery rhymes give sounds the sound of sense –
darkly, as the children run shrieking from the witch's house,
or in tracers of light as the frog turns into the prince.
Poets are those who, in time, pick up from the world
eccentric wavelengths in tune with their own translations of,
say, the heart, a river, or buds unfurling
suddenly in spring. They believe in implication –
or, like that Portuguese person, are in hiding, becoming
a secret orchestra playing a symphony for one.

A Brief Treatise on Rhyme
(for Jonathan and Seema)

Some rhymes are best defined
as bilateral fibrillation –
like chill-out and stress
day and night
sun and ice

Others are hard to divine
even by auscultation –
like lung and buttress
chest and quartzite
heart and gneiss

Some of the good ones incline
to simple ingurgitation –
like fruits of the press
whipped cream and egg-white
curry and rice

But the best all combine
confinement and liberation –
like home and happiness
duet and delight
marriage and licence

His Master's Voice

Odourless, all presence reduced
to sound, every movement
to the round and round
inroading O of obedience –
and a bent stick at the centre
no dog will ever reach.

All this the cocked ear
hears from the blaring cone
as, patiently, he waits
for the hiss of the final
criss-crossing, shiny grooves –
for the arm lifted, the return.

Singer Asleep

Sometimes she feels choked
by air and pressure,
that tautness, the way
coloratura
gets hold of her and shakes her

But now she lies out, bedded
in goth velvet
as if the hinged
lid of an étui
might shut her away into darkness

An instrument quite worn out,
she dreams of nothing,
not even hotels,
schedules or her agent
struggling on a poor line

Only rest can retune her,
return her to her hearers
to risk once more
such self-possession,
such exposure of the soul

Coconuts in the Cardiac Ward

Hospital more or less darkness, and all
with a one way or another faulty heart,
laid out in a row

Finally, with someone's nebuliser off,
and the voice shouting *No!* from a side-room giving up,
more or less quiet

And then, from the eighty-three year old builder
in the next-door bed, a single line sung
happily in his sleep –

There they are, all standing in a row –
and yes, somehow they are, cupped awry
in their red and white holders

Various as humans, and each hairy fruit
at the mercy, its white milk cocooned in the night
like a long-held hope

Going Home

He heard from behind his head
the burly anaesthetist calling
for the atropine

And the high ceiling of the ward
began to cut out neatly
in square blocks

She came to him, dressed in white
like a nurse or perhaps a bride
instructed to assist

Over her shoulder, he saw
a narrowing tunnel, all
that must be relinquished

He could imagine coming to,
signing the discharge papers,
drinking tea, going home

But not how to erase
her image, or forget the snap
of her bright shears

Fourfold

Elizabeth Blackadder's *Still Life with Lily and Flute*

In this scoured country
the lily's trumpets
hang slackly,
mere doodles in air.

Neither does the flute
utter: and a bird,
uncertain, stands
mute, half in,
half out of its cage.

Yet music persists
as a prayer in waiting –
as the tunes locked
in the flute, in the dream
of the bird rising
to sing and fly free.

Max Ernst's *Petrified Town*

The weight of the moon
lumbers the ashen sky
its borrowed light
too neatly described
above the dark drift

Every squeak
of the night strains for meaning
in the blacked-out comb
where sweetness rots
in the clogged wells and ditches

Over the reef
looms a stone silence
the slow burn
of unfinished business
or an unfulfilled longing

Howard Hodgkin's *Rain*

As if, turning away
from a pleasant enough chat,
you happen to see, arrested
in the window's view-finding frame,
an entire season blurred
by tears – and sunk somewhere
in a swell of sea and grass,
the sense of a thread lost.
Rich drapes. Colours
that work together to ward
the implications of silence.
Or the sudden drench of knowing
that nothing will ever be the same.

Bridget Riley's *Metamorphosis*

Here it is, in black and white –
the optic nerve seduced into playing
a blinder. Pressures out of sight
mill all images back to latency,
the mind's series, treacherous and true.

Yet definitions are at their sharpest
when speeding towards the point where disks
of silver and black throng to the mesh
of something like judgement, then a remix
of tried perceptions, making them new –
as, say, the image of holes in a colander
themselves drained away; or a swarming stream
of fish-eggs; or a geometer's world
of ciphers somehow unhooked from time,
an eternity made of in betweens.

Now you don't see it, now you don't –
the invisible ink which you know is there,
the oxygen of desire, which can't
be denied; that gasp of mortal love, or
the momentary gift of all its meanings.

Quanta

(for Elizabeth)

Entering a Church

The way a child rests its head
against a parent; the laughing delight
of letting the body's whole weight be propped
against the steady push of a gale;
the way in which water always accepts
our surrender, converting the sinking heart
to a loose lullaby drift –
there was something of all this
beyond the snap of the lifted latch,
the door leaning into almost silence
where each window, each harvest berry
glowed, exalted by our attention;
when, in the slow beat of the clock,
came love's double move away from dead centre.

Driving Back

At two days short of the shortest day,
belted into place like puppet pilots
facing the oncoming stars, we returned
to the sweet city. Ahead of us,
its dreaming aspirations had blackened
to cardboard flats against the blazing
indifference of the sinking sun –
and we entered into a silence
that comprehended the light streaming
from the rim of every minim moment,
from each quick intake of breath;
and which knew how to cherish the luck of sharing
the singularity that is
the seedling dream of endless galaxies.

Divisions on a Ground

It is, on one level,
what light, shade and a high
skin colour have arranged
unforgettably along
either side of your cheekbones;
on another, something that makes
my heels suddenly heavy
with the traction of glue – as if
a hand had reached from below
ground to grab my ankle,
making it all but impossible
to turn and go. It is
the number of times that knowledge
cannot go into love.

At the Full

The night before leaving home: a case
packed, its static model of order
a snapshot out of time pre-empting
any declension of departure

Sleep is a distant dream. Below,
the city lies supine and silent beneath
a full moon with attendant clouds,
hypnotised by falling light

Concertinas of terrace houses,
roadways widened by emptiness,
the river lying low in its channel,
the set pieces of surrounding hills

So, too, when I let the curtain
drop, and turn back to darkness,
my heart-trace image of you stays,
constant as all the shine outside

Foxglove

Gawky, almost,
the narrow pagoda
of clustering bells –
conspicuous,
attention-seeker.
And gets it doubly,
also from the humble-bee's
looping approach.
It crawls over
the flecked threshold –
intimate, veiled
in purple. Falls
silent, reaches
for loot.
As well
that your other yield
steadies the over-
excited heart.

White Carnations

Flesh-flowers, eyelets
crisp as tutus
yet denying elegance –
such dusty silver
on their stems
and weak leaves
such arthritic knobbles

Everything depends
on the blooms themselves
in their plump holders –
the way they appear
sudden as a trick
surprising as feathers
that sprout from bamboo

Their brightness seems
to demand a scent
stronger than they offer –
but they command
occasions easily
rising to corsage
nosegay or lapel

And even after
their weakest buds
have hung their heads –
when their fœtid water
has been tipped away
their browning frills
still haunt death

Myosotis

(remembering Jill Balcon)

Sometimes it presented as the sleekest
of pale blue soaps, to be held,
stroked and inclined towards
as you snuffed the heady scent;
sometimes it might have been
no more than a grace note sung
as part of a Latin litany
compiled for a gardener's roll-call.

From the single tulip selected
for endearment, to the richest of puddings
or fumy marinades, the music
of words, or your cottage steeped
in the notes of your favourite pianist,
it was all one – your oath
of allegiance to appetite, sworn
like a trouper, with tears and laughter.

And sometimes it could seem as simple
as the stem held loosely by a woman
in a portrait painted long ago,
precise in its detail as her headdress,
where each stitch dints the material;
and memorable – like the lingering
waft of the soap that stays
on the very tips of the fingers.

An Exchange of Gifts
(for Erica)

It is in my dreams and in fact
that I cup the back of your head
in my hand, as if you were wounded
and about to utter. Your hair
cropped short, your neck
that seems so fragile a stem
have become, across the divides
of time, gifts that rise
clear of change and chance –
as the moon, neither new nor old,
can lift clarion clear,
its single shine refreshing
as a gush of water that is
poured onto parted lips.

In Praise of Limes

Thin-skinned but tough
they are on the side
of intensity – compact,
they test the knife

Cut in two, they show
how light has bled
into their heart
as a green glow

The taste has a scantling
of sherbet, almost,
of a perfume freighted
with an acid tang

And even at the finish
when the rind discolours,
something still eludes
exact definition –

Like bluebells in a blur,
or the way coriander
can quiver the eye
like oncoming tears

Near Postbridge

The stone fold
embossed on the tilt
of the moor offers
enclosure and escape
as roughly equal
propositions
where space stands
in for time

The hours stay penned
in a green clock-face
the bleating minutes
scatter across
the low wall
through the death-defying
mid-yellow of gorse

Not at the Eleventh Hour

Quiescence – the moon
flirts in a shift of cloud,
the night-blossom hangs
heavy, with the weight
of a breast held
in the lover's hand

Streetlights steady,
cars slewed to a halt –
here, now,
again, the river
smuggles seawards
hidden in its flood

And let not praise
be the qualified, almost too late,
propped deathbed cry,
but uttered whenever
the secret opens,
broad as sunlight –

From the skein of the water,
from the yaffle's unshared joke,
or the robin of the bush,
tilted in attendance
on the air: from each
contingency that gives
love its bearings

Old Men Walking

Things are not what they seem. Breathless,
one halts abruptly, pats his pockets
with flapping hands, in search of something
he knows isn't there. Another, wincing,
stops to look across or up, proving
he is just taking in the view or the weather.

But once, on Bonehill Down in autumn,
when stillness had settled in grey and green
on the knuckled moor; and once again
at Hartland Quay, with all the gold
draining from the land to the ocean's shimmer,
I saw an old man stopped in his tracks –

Not by any transaction of pride,
but as if he had glimpsed, from the lookout
of his own ghost, the world as it could be –
the hard-won silence, the rich smelt-houses
of shine: and himself, in the pure astonishment
of facing what he knew couldn't be there.

Goethe's *Traveller's Nightsong*

Over every peak,
still air,
in every treetop
you sense scarcely
a breath of wind spilling:
in the wood, no fledgling song.
Be patient, before long
you, too, will be still.

Leopardi's *The Infinite*

Always I have cherished this secluded hill
and no less this hedgerow that so largely
blocks any view of the far horizon.
But as I sit, intent, it is the endless
spaces of the beyond with their more than human
silences, their fathomless utter calm
that my mind conjures, spaces in which
the heart all but sinks. And hearing the wind
riffle the hedge-leaves, I find myself
measuring that infinite silence against
its voice: and I recall the eternal,
and the dead seasons, and the quick of the moment
with all its sounds. So it is that my thinking
drowns amid this vastness: and sweet
it is to founder in such a sea.

Boxed Heads in Brittany

Niched and kennelled – to each
a little house, with space
for an eye to peep out through
a single, heart-shaped hole:
maisonettes of memory,
an estate of double detacheds
each waving a cross
like an aerial at the rooftop.

No need to ask *Ubi sunt?* –
They are safely home and dry,
the capital parings of Jenny
Nédéric and Doctor Trober,
and Father Nébout de la Brousse,
sixty-second bishop of Léon:
all with their sockets staring
into the dark north aisle.

A Field near Trémolat

I have carried it long enough
in my head, that blazing lozenge
seen years ago,
tipping from left to right
towards the sunlit river,
crammed with bright barley

I could learn to do without it
and whatever was immanent there,
but it stays, lit
from within, and made brighter
by the dark screening trees –
all the more unsettling
for its lack of narrative,
or a gate, a way out or in

Annunciation

To anyone looking out beyond
the feverish noise of the city, across
the valley with its twisting path and the lone
cypress close to the bridge, it would be
nothing – a small aperture, one
of several visible in the north wall
of an admittedly fine palazzo.

No hint of the room where a woman
is confronting a creature with wings that crowd
the chequered floor tiles. Behind the lily
he holds, an arch frames the valley with its bridge
and a nearby tree, and the path twisting
up to the distant city on its ridge –
the world as a miniature nailed to the wall.

A Visit in June
(St Bartholomew's Chapel, Rodhuish)

In the purged light of limewash
clear windows give
onto silence: the wing of the door
opens to candour, God
in an element cool as north.

Here, all that is wrought
has become one and simple,
guileless as the saint standing
under the fig-tree, or the blessing
wrestled from an angel at dawn.

And even time is rendered
simply, as a single stand
of chrysanthemums, and two sprays
of pinks in small brass vases
set on facing sills.

Outside, a lattice-work
of birdsong and shadow. Grass-fumes
lift from the unlettered precinct:
in the fields, the buried seed
aims at brilliant cloud.

Thinking of Klee again

The fish are not biting today –
neither the great golden ones
nor the iridescent shoals
on which the light wavers
as they twitch first this,
then that way.

The boat pivots idly, slurs
with almost magnetic reluctance
like a fairground ride running down:
the angler's line crimps,
lies, a broken hairspring,
flat on the surface.

There is no end to the bliss
of tracing anagrams of magic:
and look – nosing into
the gloom under the keel,
glides a hitherto unknown
magnificent red fish.

Treading Water

gift   Today the sea is open-handed –
from its calm, murmuring angles,
its pure ultramarine,
the light fractures
in sparks, sparks, sparks

*

slack   Flatlining surface, playing dead –
as if the driving
coulter of the keel
were a scalpel drawn
across veined depths

*

fishy   They hang in the flows
a glinting cloud
that barely quivers
waiting for the moment
at which to about turn

*

treading Keep pedalling
water   keep your head
above water
keep treading

keep heading
upwards
keep your hands spread
keep treading

keep steady
keep studying
the stars, keep treading,
stay where you are

*

221

ear   The ocean listens to itself –
to the sudden out-of-nowhere chuckle
that flourishes in its labyrinth,
to the way its overfalls
tune themselves to silence

*

either/or   Innocent of curse
and blessing, the sea
stalls on the sand,
or drives its toppling wall
miles inland

*

nocturne   Sea-fire streaming downward,
contented engines, lights
rocked over darkness...there are times
when the moon seals the water
and any dream might be true

Overfalls

Like a sweet dream,
those endless versions
of the sea you once harboured –
the muscular calm
of its blue indifference,
the glister of the sun
hammering its furrows,
or the heave of spume
splayed in a gale.

Here there is only
the evidence of a strength
bent against itself,
ominous as the fever
of a dark squall –
broken narratives,
scurries rasping
the hull, surfaces
overlaid with denial.

Undertow

Always hidden,
it is water channelled
to a true direction –
the plaited twists
of the currents make
their moves in a way
mysterious as prayer,
pure intention
freed from appearance.

The swirl of it gathers
deep under,
moves across
the balancing fish,
the kingdoms of coral
where polyps die –
more alluring,
more sustaining
than can ever be known.

A Leaf Falling

The stem snaps off, brittle
as a wafer – another sycamore
half-star on its way to collapsing
its yellow ribs on the ground.

Not yet: as it slaloms the air
it calls the whole valley to attention –
the glacier's green withheld ghosts,
the breaker's yard of the moraine,
the peaks fat with sunlight.

They attend to a silence which covers
all the leaf's lilting fall:
long enough to contain
the cry of a newborn child
crossing the threshold into
the dazzle, the shadows beyond.

Sleet at Christmas

Slut of winter, needling,
insistent, it fingers the window,
its slow sago crawls
uncertainly down the pane –
a middling failure, it seems,
of rain, of snow.

It draws its grey curtain
across the valley, all but hiding
the scar of the empty track,
the bare, flailing trees –
its high drifts pelt
over miles of air.

When it clears, an east wind
rattles the darkening hills.
A star slides out. Coal-smoke
squirms up, acrid: a distant
radio sings. Later,
the usual snow.

Overwintering

Journeying between
two suns at their closest
to the line clarifies
a point of departure –
the fields where sunlight
softened the stubble,
when the corn was already
scutched and stowed
and the black-bright weave
of the wood still dense
with late leaf-shade.

Ahead, the crocuses
primed for spring
ward their whites,
their light purples –
but long before then,
at a turning-point
where, it is said,
the sun stands still,
a family is waiting,
parents with a child
pale in his stripped innocence.

Ghostings

1

Fallen fruit of the flesh,
fruit of the broken word,
bright and brindled, you weigh
much more in the hand
than on the bough.

                    And yet,
I once more smell the dew
and rain, and relish versing.
Meanwhile, the seas rise
and the ideograms of God fail.

*

In an empty church by the Thames
an impervious stained-glass angel
unfurls a scroll – *Behold*
thy mother as once she was

Thy mother now reduced
to a fine sift of ash,
surprisingly dark, that slides
with a sigh from the plastic jar

Her given-up ghost settles
with a brief puff of dust
(and think of thy cousin also,
her ashes dispersed among bluebells)

Reader, the book of the world
is closing, however slowly,
against you. Be quick and thankful
and ignore the lives of the poets

*

O saisons! O châteaux!
Quelle âme est sans défaut?

You see them set on ridges,
fronted by a deer-park or fountains;
or as white turrets rocketing
up from a screening forest –
mausolea of money, *belles îles*
of the status quo. And round them
parade the ghosts
                    of the tetrarchs
who once shared the year between them,
now no more real
than abraded tapestry flowers.

As to the cure of souls –
in weather like interference
which never stops, there are figures
beyond number, falling;
and soldiers, their clothing rolled
in blood; and the drowned innocents.
There is what can be done
                    and what cannot,
and the old longing for quiescence,
for requests simple as those
of a child who doesn't care.

O châteaux! O saisons!
Quelle âme n'a pas ses raisons?

    *

For the word's illuminations
read the fluorescent image
and the all-seeing lens that shrieks
in from space to examine
your back yard.
                    And the flesh?
Do not forbear to examine
the crematorium curtain
diaphanous as lingerie
and light as dust.

2

Even that child filled with sad thoughts
at the moment of launching *a boat frail*
as a May butterfly, did not dream
of how a ship might one day be hauled
out of its element entirely, and find
beneath its iron-shod keel not the rasp
of shingle but greasy city cobbles,
the hull not handed along on the tide
but steered on rails.
                    It is more than halfway
to death: the houses stare it down.
Ahead, nothing but the dry dock
of history, the museum's echoing halls.

Yet it will have the better of those haulers.
Into the dull database of the future
it will smuggle the log of imagined voyages –
night-time secrets, the compass rose
blossoming, the duty officer's features
unearthly, uplit by the binnacle's glow.
Then, muffled by the wheelhouse glass,
the *douf! douf!* of the bows as they plunge
and rear and slew:
                    the brief sizzle
of spray falling back and, at the edge
of the dark, the loom of lights implying
the first nudge of the harbour wall.

        *

On deck someone is not
drowning but waving with flags:

D — *keep clear of me, I*
am having difficulty manœuvring

Afterwards, F — *I am disabled,*
communicate with me

C — Charlie — *yes*
N — November — *no*

Tick one box only

*

Some promises are only to be made
too late, from the end of the wharf,
or through breath-smeared glass
as the train pulls out.

No frantic tapping on the sealed window,
no desperate run the length of the deck
till the deck runs out
can alter this.

The great steamer curves gracefully
towards the horizon: the bulk of the train
diminishes to a single
eyeblink of light.

And in the silence that succeeds parting,
it is often the same questions that hang
like undispersed smoke
in the still air:

what, really, was intended? What
did either want? And why is sadness
too frequently tinged
with a sense of relief?

*

Impossible also to forget
that zone of shadow
along the estuary
where the massy wood
tilts to the water,
its shoreline fringe
sheared by the salt –
where, if you crouched,
the dinghy could just slip in.

Earlier, when the straining hull
heeled too far over
and the sea raced past then
over the gunwale
you learnt exactly
what was meant by
a moment of truth:
how its sudden shock
came up to slap you dizzy.

And now that the child is asking
with urgent redundancy
What name are you called?
it is those same
images that recur:
of refuge, exposure,
secrecy, glare –
words that rattle
the cage, but are hardly answers.

3

Daughters, you were born
from the twinning of despair
and intense longing –
startling instances
of the gene that dreams
the dream is fact.

Words fly to you
daily, you are giddy
with the sound of their spinning,
you love all absurdities,
all that distorts
the mirrors of meaning.

And even now
as you learn what comes
in the guise of apples,
spindles, trolls
and gluttonous ogres,
you know what you know:

how magic works,
how the wolves and the witches
will always lose out,
and the lost slipper
never fail
to find its twin.

And the heart of the forest,
though dark, is alive
with any number
of princely riders,
their saddlebags stuffed
with ever-after kisses.

Even the word
that rhymes with breath
is no more, on your lips,
than a brief experiment
in sound, nothing
to the claims of now.

Seamless, the waking
dreams of children,
in which elisions
are endless and meanings
multiple, each name
an eponym of delight:

where a handful of air
is a real gift;
a balloon, a posy;
a half-bitten biscuit,
a bridge; and forever
lasts less than an hour.

But this, too,
is a dream – I sit
with a child either side
and have the view
they never will quite
have of themselves –

the head streamlined
as a cyclist's helmet,
the almost egg-like
narrowing of the skull
between back
and occipital front.

One blonde,
one brunette
– and each with hair
that streams perfectly
down from the high
ridge of the crown.

Thinking of their future
admits hope
as much as fear –
it is the present
that summons their siblings,
the suffering ghost-children:

whose troubled eyes
reflect war, illness,
the lupine triumph
of adults; the forests
hushed and dead;
themselves, coffined in darkness.

4

There must be a last time
for everything – missing the bus,
making tea or love,
writing more poems, even
for gazing into the future

Whenever he went away
he left a single sheet
of A4 under the scrutiny
of the desk-light, as if its blankness
could ward off the word GONE.

Meanwhile, the curtain goes on
rising and falling, although
the theatre is fast rotting.
Onstage, the spirit of opera –
over-ripe music and the surtitles
stuck at *but it is too late.*

Perhaps poems, in the way
that a river glides onward
even when hidden by trees,
are always there, although
you may not always glimpse them.

Are they also what wake you
in the night, with your heart battering
your chest, and your mind wondering
whether or not you heard
a door slam downstairs?

Even now, the poem wants
to arrest the malleable word,
to witness to something more
than the hauntings of hope – to become
new, singular fruit
that gleams on the cankered tree.

Index of titles and first lines

(Titles are in italics, first lines in roman type

239